NAVAJO
—PLACE NAMES—

AN OBSERVER'S GUIDE

COMPILED AND WRITTEN BY ALAN WILSON
WITH GENE DENNISON, NAVAJO CONSULTANT

FOREWORD BY N. SCOTT MOMADAY

Jeffrey Norton Publishers
Guilford, Connecticut

Other Navajo programs available from Audio-Forum:

Breakthrough Navajo: An Introductory Course, 2 cassettes, (3 hr.) and 234-page text, #AFNV10

Speak Navajo: Intermediate, 2 cassettes, (2 hr.) and 180-page text, #AFNV20

Laughter: The Navajo Way (Humorous Stories of the Navajo) 1 cassette (80 min.) and 143-page text, #AFNV30.

Basic Medical Navajo, 1 cassette (1 hr.) and 141-page text, #AFNV40

Seasons of a Navajo (in English and Navajo), 1 VHS cassette (60 min.), #V72300.

Navajo Nights, 1 cassette, approximately 50 minutes, #C11314

Stargazer, 1 cassette, approximately 60 minutes, #C11315

Navajo Place Names
An Observer's Guide

cover photograph: Pyramid Rock, New Mexico. Photograph by Kaye Wilson

ISBN 0-88432-824-4   text and cassette
ISBN 0-88432-825-2   text only

Published by Jeffrey Norton Publishers, Inc.
On-the-Green, Guilford, Connecticut 06437-2635

For Kaye

Foreword

Where language touches the earth, there is the holy, there is the sacred. In our deepest intelligence we know this: that names and being are indivisible. That which has no name cannot truly be said to exist, to be. That which bears a name bears being as well. **I have a name; therefore I am.** And of course there is a wonderful particularity in names. If we are speaking of place, which is (or ought to be) a fundamental concept in our lives, the particularity is critical. We know who we are (and where we are) only with reference to the things about us, the points of reference in both our immediate and infinite worlds, the places and points among which we are born, grow old, and die. There is in this simple cartology the idea of odyssey. And in odyssey there is story. Nothing is older than story in our human experience. Nothing appeals more to our human being.

Where is Haske?
Haske has gone to Gallup.
Ah, Na'nízhoozhí, the place of the bridge.
Aoo', the old bridge over the Rio Puerco. It has long been a meeting place for the Diné.
When I was a child at Ch'ínílį I thought of Na'nízhoozhí as one of the great cities of the world.
And so it is. There is no world without the lights of Na'nízhoozhí. Haske has gone there to meet a man from Naakaii Tó, a man who owns fine horses, they say.
There is a story in that, daats'í.
We are speaking of horses. We are telling a story.

The Navajos say of their language, Diné bizaad, that it is endless. I realized the truth of this saying when I studied the language with Alan Wilson in the early seventies. Although I am not Navajo, I had lived at Shiprock, Tuba City, and Chinle as a child. I heard the sounds of the Navajo language, its rhythms and inflections, its cadences and pitches, at a fortunate time, when my ear was more alive to the spoken word than it had ever been or would ever be again. When I met Alan and came into the immediate presence of the Navajo language again, I found that Diné bizaad was alive in my memory and in my hearing.

What a joy it was to enter again into that particular dimension of sound and meaning! But I knew next to nothing about the logical structure of the language. The great grammar of Navajo was completely new to me, and yet I had the advantage of knowing something about its oral underpinnings. With Alan's help, I began to perceive the patterns and geometries of Navajo; I began to see that the Navajo language is indeed endless. Diné bizaad is a kind of definition of the infinite.

One day a remarkable thing happened. I was driving from Gallup north towards Kayenta. Soon there appeared on the side of the road a young Navajo hitchhiker, certainly not an unusual figure then and there. I pulled over, and he climbed into the car. He nodded his thanks in a very jovial manner. He was clearly grateful to be given the lift, and he seemed to be at home in the world. I started talking to him in my meager, broken Navajo. He was amused, I'm sure, but he was gracious. He did not want to embarrass me; even so he could not help drawing me quickly beyond my depth. But I had a basic question: Éi haash hoolyé?—What is the name of that place, or, how is that place called? I must have asked this question a hundred times, and a hundred times he had the name of the place I pointed out.

Éi haash hoolyé?
Tóhaach'i'.
Éi haash hoolyé?
Tsé Awé'é.

I was amazed. It soon became clear to me that this man was indeed at home. He was eminently familiar with the places that defined him. Not only did he know them, as we know the images of cityscape, horizon, and, if we are truly blessed, the stars in the night sky, but he knew their names!

One day Alan and I drove to Monument Valley, Tsé Bii' Ndzisgaii, and camped for the night in a box canyon, under an overhanging red cliff that rode slowly in the sky at every hour of the day and night. It seemed always to be in motion, and it was something for the imagination, something for the hungry spirit. Beyond the mouth of our canyon there were the Three Sisters, Tsé Yaa'áhí, those slender monuments that seem to defy age and gravity, the statuary of an ancient deity. Above us were the brightest stars I have ever seen. We built a fire and cooked an incomparable meal. The good-smelling smoke of our fire rose slowly upon the incline of the great wall leaning over us, great, mythic shadows rippling there as if in the telling of a primal story. We slept deeply, deeply in that place. The next morning we awoke and breakfasted in wonder of the world. Then we climbed to a window in the end of the canyon, a wind-shaped opening high above the canyon floor. And through the window we saw the vast valley below, reaching out across the long, ascending reach of the continent. In the distance under us there were two men on horseback, Navajo men going in slow motion towards story, towards a memory that would keep to my mind forever. They were singing a riding song, and the song rose up to us with the clarity of a bell.

Somewhere in the back of my mind I knew then and there that the essential things of the world and the universe were and are in place, in place. They are fixed forever in their names.

N. Scott Momaday
Tucson, 1994

Shik'éí kééhat'įįdi áadi tádísháah
Kinłichí'ídi áadi tádísháah
Iiná nineezii bee hooghan bii' tádísháah
Hózhóonii bee hooghan bii' tádísháah
Sạ'ạh naaghái, bik'eh hózhóón bik'ehgo tádísháah
Atiin hózhónigo yisháał

I wander there where my people dwell
I wander there at the house of red earth and rocks
I wander within the house made of long life
I wander within the house made of beauty
I wander along the path of long life and happiness
I shall go on wandering the trail in beauty.

Navajo Blessingway Song

Preface

The place names in this book represent the harvest of many years of cooperative endeavor. The names have been gathered from Navajo sheepherders, ranchers, hitchikers, and from other offhand encounters with Navajos around the far reaches of Navajo country, as well as from the extant literature. The present collection attempts to be generously illustrative in terms of the most widely known and used names in everyday Navajo discourse. As such, it contains most of the names shown on the map at the front of the book. The map, titled *Diné Bikéyah: Navajo Land,* includes cities, villages, post offices, and trade centers within the Navajo reservation boundary. The Navajo penchant for widespread naming of rocks, trees, creeks, canyons, washes, and, in general, almost every spot is well known. Therefore, there are many names in this compilation that will not be on any map or in any compendium in existence. And the collection, because of the density of names throughout the reservation, is necessarily representative rather than exhaustive.

In whatever conversations one may have in Navajo with a native, place names form a prominent place in the structure of the discourse. "My family lived near Tséyaaniichii' (Where Red Rocks Come Down and Stop). We moved a lot, to Tóhaach'i' (Water is Scratched Out), to Mạ'ii Tééh Yítłizhí (Where Coyote Fell Into Deep Water), and then over to T''iists'óóz Ńdeeshgizh (Slim Cottonwood Pass). *T''iists'óóz Ńdeeshgizhísh hwíiní'į́?* Do you know T''iists'óóz Ńdeeshgizh?"

Keith Basso, in his splendid book *Western Apache Language and Culture, Essays in Linguistic Anthropology,* quotes Harry Hojier (personal communication, 1973) on the Navajo: "Even the most minute occurrences are described by Navajos in close conjunction with their physical settings, suggesting that unless narrated events are *spatially anchored* their significance is somehow reduced and cannot be properly assessed." Basso writes, in discussing Apache place names (and here, the word *Navajo* is legitimately substitutable for *Western Apache* or *Apache*): "Something else contributes to the common use of placenames in Western Apache communities, however, and that, quite simply, is that Apaches enjoy using them." This statement precisely describes the gusto the Navajos display in the use of their own place names, because they avow, just as their linguistic Athabascan cousins the Apaches do, that "...those names are good to say."

Navajo place names may be arbitrarily categorized into names with verbs and those without verbs. More specific subclassifications can then be drawn from these two general headings:

Names with verbs, natural phenomena, motion or movement implied
Ch'inílį: ch'í - *out, outward* nílį - *it flows* (it flows out - Chinle, Arizona).

Names with verbs, fixed natural formations or entities
Tsé Ndoolzhaaí: tsé - *rock* ndoolzha(a) - *it extends downward in jagged form* í - *the place* (the place where it extends downward in jagged form - Dinosaur Canyon, Arizona).

Names with verbs, man-made entities
Atoo' Ditsxizí: atoo' - *soup* ditsxiz - *it shakes, trembles* í - *the place* (the place where soup shakes - Casa San Martin, Gallup, New Mexico).

Names with verbs, historical
Naakaii Deíchahí: Naakaii - *Mexican(s)* deícha - *they cried, wept* (h)í - *the place* (the place where the Mexicans cried - near Ganado, Arizona).

Names with verbs, mythological
Yé'iitsoh Bidił Niníyęęzh: yé'iitsoh - *a giant, a large supernatural being* bidił - *its blood* niníyęęzh - *it stopped flowing* (the giant's blood stopped flowing - Anzac, New Mexico).

Names with verbs, for persons
Hashké Neiniihii: hashké - *he is angry, fierce* neiniih - *he distributes it or them, metes out* ii - *the one* (one who metes out anger, or distributes it or them angrily or fiercely Hoskaninii Mesa, Arizona).

Names with verbs, for animals
Mą'ii Tééh Yítłizhí: mą'ii - *coyote* tééh - *deep water* yítłizh - *he, she fell in* í - *the place* (where the coyote fell into deep water - Coyote Canyon, New Mexico).

Names without verbs, natural phenomena, motion or movement implied
Są́ Bitooh: są́ - *old age* bitooh - *its river* (old age river - the San Juan River).

Names without verbs, fixed natural formations or entities
Tsoodził: tsoo (tsoo') - *tongue* dził - *mountain* (tongue mountain - Mount Taylor, New Mexico).

Names without verbs, man-made entities
Ayahkinii: ayah - *underground* kin - *house(s)* ii - *the ones* (underground house people - Hopi Villages, Arizona).

Names without verbs, historical
Naashashí: (a)naa' - *enemy, enemies* shash - *bear* í - *the one(s)* (bear enemies, enemies like bears - Santa Clara Pueblo, New Mexico).

Names without verbs, mythological
Tł'iishtsoh Baghan: tł'iishtsoh - *big snake* baghan - *his, her, its home* (Big Snake's home - Black Rock, Arizona).

Names without verbs, for persons

Náyaaseęsí: ná (anaa') - *eye* yaa - *beneath, under* sęęs - *wart* i - *the one* (the one with a wart under the eye - Joseph City, Arizona).

Names without verbs, for animals

Giní Bit'oh: giní - *hawk* bit'oh - *its nest* (hawk's nest - Kinbito, New Mexico).

It is apparent from the above examples that Navajo place names are highly descriptive in a pictorial sense. As such, they are powerful descriptors of land formations, mesas, canyons, buttes, of colors of rocks, of bodies of water, and of places named for people and animals. They enable the Navajo to see the places as pictures.

There are dialectical and ideolectical differences in the pronunciation, and thus the spelling, of some of the names. The word for *rock* is characteristically *tsé*, but also *ché*. For a gap that comes downward one might hear either *nihodeeshgizh* or *nahodeeshgizh*. A mountain may be called *tsis* as well as *sis*. Navajos may dispute the name of a certain place. People inevitably disagree about how places are called. One sometimes hears this kind of comment: "Some people call it *Kéyah Nihoneel'ání*, but I say *Tółá Dah Siyíní*. Well, I guess some of them call it that, too." Or, "My uncle says *Yódí Dził* rather than *Yódí Dziil*, so I asked a medicine man and he said both ways are correct." It is also an intriguing point that the exact meaning, or concept inferred, of some of the names has been lost in time. As only one example, the Carrizo Mountains in Arizona have the name *Dził Náhoozilii*, carrying interpretations as widely varied as *turning mountain, whirling mountain, mountain that gropes around, mountain that turns or whirls gathering, and mountain surrounded by mountains.*

While most names stand on their own, unrelated in meaning to the non-Navajo term or only tangentially related, some Navajo names are fairly direct translations of non-Navajo names and vice versa: Bear's Ears, Utah as *Shashjaa'*, or Bird Spring, Arizona as *Tsídii To'í*. It is additionally interesting to note that the names of places on maps and road signs are often highly inaccurate renditions of the Navajo terms. For example, the Navajo name *T'iis Názbąs* is rendered everywhere as *Teec Nos Pos*, *Ch'ínílí* as *Chinle*, *Ch'óshgai* as *Chuska*, and so forth.

The place names in this book are arranged, non-Navajo name first, in alphabetical order. A gloss of the etymological components of the Navajo name is next, followed by a roughly literal translation of the complete Navajo term. Then, a brief commentary notes historical or other pertinent data and provides information regarding location, using other geographical places, with their Navajo names in parentheses, as referents. Distances between points are given wherever possible. In most cases quick reference may be made through the use of the map, but as was stated earlier, there are many names that do not appear on any map of the area. There are also some names on the map that are not in this collection of Navajo place names.

The accompanying cassette recording, read by native speakers of Navajo, encompasses the pronunciation guide and the entire text of place names. Each non-Navajo name is read once and each Navajo term twice. The alphabetical arrangement of the names permits ready access to any name on the cassette.

The foreword, written by Pulitzer prize-winning novelist N. Scott Momaday, greatly enriches and distinguishes this book. Momaday, a Kiowa (Káawa) who grew up among the Navajos and who deeply values their language and culture, instinctively intuits the subtleties as well as the mysteries that link Navajo language and place. This intuition is evident throughout his text. I can think of no one more fitting or capable of creating a foreword to this work and I was elated by his enthusiastic acceptance of my invitation to do the writing. "I want a crack at it," he said. I am enduringly grateful to him, a highly esteemed friend of many years, for the significance his words give to the book.

I also gratefully acknowledge the following staff of *The Indian Trader* for their vital contributions to this volume: Martin Link, photographer and southwest historian, for his photographs, which add lustre and integrity to the immensely detailed text, and for his screening of the historicity and other minutiae in the commentaries; Bill Donovan for his critically important work in producing the Navajo-English glossary as well as for his troubleshooting skills in general; Ron Velasco for his ever reliable and energetic efforts, often beyond the bounds of normal working hours, in doing the detailed and difficult job of typesetting and composition of each item of the text and for the extra hard hours spent in correcting proofed copy. I am also indebted to the following people for their indispensable work in the production of the book: Gene Dennison and Cecilia Held, native speakers of Navajo, for their polished tape recording of the Navajo names in the book; Chuck Simms for his sound-engineering expertise in producing high quality master tapes of the readings; the Rights and Permission Committee of the University of Oklahoma Press for granting permission to use the maps from James M. Goodman's book *The Navajo Atlas: Environments, Resources, People, and History of the Diné Bikéyah;* Kaye Wilson and John Riley for their comprehensive proofing of the materials; Robert Young, William Morgan, and the late Father Berard Haile whose pioneering work in Navajo linguistics (see references) are a *sine qua non* for the undertaking of most projects involving the Navajo language; Ella Roanhorse Morgan, Garnet Roanhorse, Roger Haley, Tony Hood, Louise Curley, Loren Toddy, and Herbert Lee, Navajos all, for providing names or access to names, as well as for other important contributions to the production of the book. And my boundless gratitude goes to the numerous other Navajos throughout the Reservation who have always so cordially talked names upon even the most casual of acquaintainships.

Alan Wilson

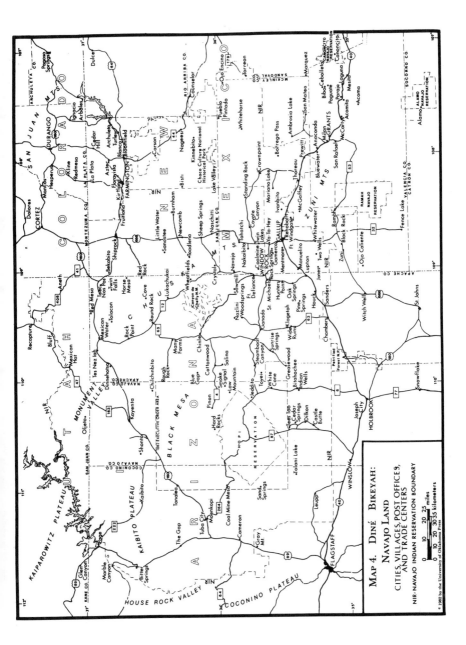

From *The Navajo Atlas: Environments, Resources, People and History of the Diné Bikeyah* by James M. Goodman. Copyright © 1982 by the University of Oklahoma Press.

From *The Navajo Atlas: Environments, Resources, People and History of the Diné Bikeyah* by James M. Goodman. Copyright © 1982 by the University of Oklahoma Press.

Guide to Navajo Pronunciation

Short Vowel Sounds

There are four basic short vowel sounds in Navajo. Short vowel sounds are represented by a single vowel letter:

a	gad *(juniper)*	dah *(up, elevated)*	Like *a* in *father*.
e	tsé *(rock)*	dego *(upward)*	Like *e* in *bed*.
i	bis *(clay)*	chizh *(firewood)*	Like *i* in *bid*.
o	tó *(water)*	dloh *(laughter)*	Like *o* in *go*.

Long Vowel Sounds

Each of the above short vowel sounds may be lengthened. A doubled vowel letter represents a longer vowel sound:

aa	saad *(word, language)*	dláád *(mold)*
ee	jeeh *(pitch)*	béésh *(iron)*
oo	tooh *(river)*	noo' *(storage pit)*
ii	siil *(steam)*	biil *(Pueblo-style dress)*

Tone

Navajo vowel sounds may be either low or high in tone. All of the Navajo words above with accent marks over the vowels are higher in tone than the words without. Tone affects meaning:

anaa' *(enemy, war)*	anáá' *(eye)*
bikee' *(her shoe, her foot)*	bikéé' *(behind her, her tracks)*

Off-Glide and On-Glide

Long Navajo vowel sounds may slide in pitch. The off-glide is indicated with an accent mark over the first vowel letter, the on-glide with the mark over the second vowel letter:

béeso *(money)*   hágoónee' *(goodbye)*

Nasalisation

Navajo vowel sounds may be nasalized. Such vowels are pronounced through the nasal passage. Nasalisation is indicated with a hook subscripted to the vowel:

sá *(old age)*   sǫ' *(star)*

Nasalisation of Navajo vowels may affect meaning:

bitsi' *(his daughter)*   bitsį' *(his flesh)*   biih *(into it)*   bįįh *(deer)*

Dipthongs

ai   hai *(winter)* neezgai *(it hurts, is painful)* Somewhat like *y* in *sky*, without the off-glide.

ao   ao' *or* aoo' *(yes)* No real English equivalent.

ei   neilé *(he carries it)* ńléidi *(over there)* Somewhat like *ay* in *may*, without the off-glide.

oi   deesdoi *(it is hot)* ayóigo *(exceedingly)* Somewhat like *ew* in *chewy*, without the off-glide.

There are slight variations on the above dipthongs when the first or second element of the sound is lengthened: Tséhootsooí *(Fort De fiance)* ligaii *(the one that is white)*

Consonants

'   e'e'aah *(west)* ha'a'aah *(east)* The symbol (') represents a glottal stop, the interval sound in the English expression *oh-oh (oh (') oh)*.

b   bis *(clay, adobe)* bááh *(bread)* A voiceless and unaspirated bilabial stop, something like *p* in *spot*.

ch'   ch'ah *(hat)* ch'osh *(bug)* Glottal closure and release from English *ch* position

d   dibé *(sheep)* sid *(scar)* A voiceless and unaspirated alveolar stop, something like *t* in *store*.

dl   dloh *(laughter)* dlááд *(mold)* Like *dl* in *paddling*.

dz   dzééh *(elk)* dziil *(strength)* Like *dz* in *adze*.

g   gad *(juniper)* deg *(up)* A voiceless and unaspirated back palatal stop, something like *k* in *skid*.

gh   baghan *(her home)* naaghá *(he, she walks about)* A voiced velar spirant, with no English equivalent. The tongue is in position to say *get*, but a slight opening between back of tongue and palate allows air to come through with voice

h   (syllable initial) hai *(winter)* há *(for him or her)* A voiceless velar spirant, something like *ch* in German *doch*.

h   (syllable final) tooh *(river)* tsékooh *(rock canyon)*

hw   hwiih *(to be satisfied)* hwáah *(whew!)* Like *wh* in *when*.

j   jádí *(antelope)* jish *(medicine pouch)*

k   kin *(house)* ké *(shoe)* An aspiraed back palatal stop, somewhat like *k* in English *kin*.

kw   kwe'é *(here)* kwá'ásiní *(relatives, friends)*

k'   k'ad *(now)* k'os *(cloud(s))* From the *k* position the back of the tongue is released from against the soft palate with a simultaneous glottal release.

l   lájish *(glove)* lą'í *(many, much)*

ł   łid *(smoke)* dił *(blood)* The tongue is in the *l* position and aspiration is lateral (along the side or sides of the tongue) without voicing.

t	tin *(ice)* tó *(water)* This sound is pronounced with aspiration. Contrast English *tin* with the first Navajo example given here. Notice that the Navajo word *tó* is pronounced with both aspiration and labialization.
t'	t'iis *(cottonwood)* bit'oh *(its nest)* Tongue (in the *t* position with tip against the alveolar ridge) and glottis are simultaneously released.
ts	tsin *(tree)* tsah (needle) Like *ts* in *bits.*
ts'	ts'in *(bone)* ts'ah *(sagebrush)* Tongue (in the *ts* position) and glottis are simultaneously released. Conrast these two examples with the ones directly above.
tł	tłah *(ointment, salve)* tłog *(a gurgling sound)* This sound is like *tl* in *Tlingit.*
tł'	tl'oh *(grass, hay)* tł'éé' *(night)* Tongue (in the *tl* position) and glottis are simultaneously released.
zh	Zhinii *(African, Black)* hózhǫ *(to be peaceful, harmonious)* Like *z* in *azure.*

The consonant sounds represented by *ch, m, n, s, sh, w, y,* and *z* are very close to their English equivalents in pronunciation.

An Observer's Guide to Navajo Place Names

Abiquiu, New Mexico: Ha'ashgizh

ha - *an upgrade* • 'ashgizh - *a cut or gap*

A gapped upgrade. This adobe settlement was built upon the site of a Tewa pueblo on the south side of the Chama river, 34 miles west of Espanola, New Mexico.

Acoma Pueblo, New Mexico: Haak'oh

This name is adapted from the native Keresan appelation of the high-mesa pueblo. In 1539 Fray Marcos de Niza called it The Kingdom of Hacus. It is some 55 miles southwest of Albuquerque (Bee'eldííldahsinil), New Mexico.

Acoma Pueblo, New Mexico: Haak'oh

Acomita, New Mexico: Tó Łání Biyáázh

tó - *water* • łání - *many* • bi - *its* • (a)yáázh - *child, offspring*

The child or offspring of many waters, or much water. The people of this pueblo are related to the Laguna (Tó Łání—Much Water) pueblo people, hence Child of Much Water. Tó Łání Biyáázh is located about three miles southeast of San Fidel (Dził Łeeshch'ihí), New Mexico.

Adah Chijiyahi Canyon, Arizona: Adah Ch'íjíyáhí

adah - *down from a height, downward* • ch'í - *out, outward horizontally*
jíyá - *someone walks (walked)* • (h)í - *the place*

The place where someone walked off of a cliff. The location is in the Monument Valley (Tsé Bii' Ndzisgaii) region.

1

Agathla Peak (El Capitan), Arizona: Aghaałá
aghaa' - *wool, fur* • łą - *much, many*

Much wool or fur. This 1500 ft. volcanic pinnacle rises from the desert some 8 miles north of Kayenta (Tó Dínéeshzhee'). The rock is visible from great distances and is a sentinel for Monument Valley (Tsé Bii' Ndzisgaii). One story is that the name originates from the custom of scraping deer hides on the coarse sides of the peak, resulting in accumulations of hair or wool about the base of the pinnacle.

Agua Sal Wash (Creek), Arizona: Tó Dík'óózh Ch'íníłí
tó - *water* • dík'óózh - *salty* • ch'í - *out, outward* • níłí - *it flows*

Salty water flowing out. The Spanish name also means *salt water*. This creek is in the Canyon de Chelly (Tséyi'), flowing northwestward near Canyon del Muerto (Ane'é Tséyi').

Alamo, New Mexico: T'iistsoh
t'iis - *cottonwood* • tsoh - *big*

Big cottonwoods. Located 40 miles south of Suanee (K'aalógii Dziil) in rugged mesa and lava country, this is the site of groups of Navajos isolated from the main Navajo reservation. The location was also known as Puertocito.

Albuquerque, New Mexico: Bee'eldííldahsinil
bee'eldííl - *a ringing sound is made with it, a bell* • dah - *up, upon* • sinil - *they lie, they are in position*

Bells that are in a high place. This term refers to bells placed on both sides of the Rio Grande River used to signal the crossing of boats ferrying people from one side to the other. Albuquerque, located on the Rio Grande River (Tó Be'áád), is the population and industrial center of New Mexico.

The American Bar, Gallup New Mexico: Haazhdiigo'í
haazhdii - *through* • go' - *stumble* • í - *the place*

The stumble-through place. This highly pictorial name alludes to the availability of both front and back doors through which the intoxicated may stumble.

Aneth, Utah: T'áá Bíích'įįdii
t'áá - *just, kind of, quite* • bii' - *in him, her, it* • ch'įįdii - *devil, ghost, evil spirit*

One who has the devil in him. Also, one who can barely get along. This term may as well be used complimentarily to one who gets things done, a go-getter. It may also designate an area that is difficult to get access to. Aneth was evidently named for a trader who was irritatingly slow at waiting on customers. It is located in extreme southeast Utah. This Navajo name is also applied to Ya-Ta-Hey, New Mexico, about 6 miles north of Gallup (Na'nízhoozhí).

Antelope Lookout, Arizona: Jádí Hádét'įįh
jádí - *antelope* • hádét'įįh - *a place from which looking out or gazing out is done, a lookout*

Literally, antelope lookout. The location is about 25 miles northeast of the northern rim of Black Mesa (Dziłíjiin).

Anzac, New Mexico: Yé'iitsoh Bidił Niniyęęzh
yé'ii - *a giant, a supernatural being* • tsoh - *large, big* • bi - *his, her, its* • dił - *blood* • nini - *a terminating or cessative particle, to stop* • yęęzh - *a stem describing the flowing of a viscous or mushy liquid over a surface.*

The giant's blood stopped flowing. The mythological heroes Nayéé' Neizgháni (Monster Slayer) and Tóbájíshchíní (Born for Water) killed Yé'iitsoh. The lava in this area is said to be the dried blood of Yé'iitsoh. Anzac is a railroad station about 8 miles southeast of Grants (Naatooh Sik'ai'í), New Mexico, on the Santa Fe Railway near the lava flow from Mt. Taylor (Tsoodził).

Asaayi, New Mexico: Asaayi'
asaa' - *bowl, pot, kettle* • yi' - *in, within*
Within the bowl. This small lake is situated on the western flank of the Chuska (Ch'óshgai) Mountains, north of Todilto (Tó Dildǫ'). It is a popular fishing spot.

Atarque, New Mexico: Tsélichíí'
tsé - *rock* • lichíí' - *red, it is red*
Red rock, rocks. This old trading center is 35 miles south of Zuni Pueblo (Naasht'ézhí). The area is marked with volcanic formations. It is also known as *Tsé Lichíí' Sikaadí* (red rocks spreading flat) and *Adáágii* (the Navajo rendition of Atarque).

Awatobi, Arizona (Hopi ruin): Táala Hooghan
táala - *flat-topped* • hooghan - *hogan or home*
A flat-topped home. These Hopi ruins are between Keams Canyon (Lók'a'deeshjin) and the Jeddito (Jádító) area. The pueblo was visited by Espejo in 1583 and by Onate in 1598. It was attacked and razed by war parties from Walpi (Deez'áají') and Mishongovi (Tsétsohk'id) in 1700.

Azansosi Mesa, Arizona: Asdzą́ą́ts'ósí
asdzą́ą́ - *woman, young woman, wife* • ts'ósí - *slender, slim*
Slender woman. The name is said to refer to Mrs. John Wetherill, wife of the southwestern explorer. The mesa is in the Monument Valley (Tsé Bii' Ndzisgaii) area.

Aztec, New Mexico: Kinteel
kin - *house, building* • teel - *wide, broad*
Wide house. Aztec is on the south bank of the Animas River, 25 miles northeast of Farmington (Tóta'). The nearby ruins, named *Kinteel* by the Navajos, were excavated between 1916 and 1924. *Kinteel* is a Navajo name designating other Anasazi ruins such as Wide Ruins south of Ganado (Lók'aanteel), Arizona and Kinteel northeast of Shonto (Shą́ą́'tóhí), Arizona.

Baby Rocks, Arizona: Tsé Awéé'é
tsé - *rock, rocks* • awéé'é (awééé') - *baby*
Rock babies, or baby rocks. This clustered rock formation is situated between Kayenta (Tó Díneeshzhee') and Dennihotso (Deinihootso), Arizona.

Baca, New Mexico: Kin Ligaai
kin - *house, building* • ligai - *it is white* • í - *the one*
White house. Baca is south of old highway 66, now I-40, some 40 miles east of Gallup (Na'nízhoozhí). *Kin Ligaai* is also the Navajo name for Canyon Diablo, Moenave, and Navajo Springs, all in Arizona, and for the San Juan and Sandia pueblos in New Mexico.

3

Bacabi, Arizona: Tł'ohchintó Biyáázh

tł'oh - *grass* • chin - *odour, smell* • tó - *water, spring* • bi - *its* •
(a)yáázh - *child, offspring*

Offspring or child of the wild onion (*allium cernuum*) spring. This Hopi village
is near Hotevilla (Tł'ohchintó), Arizona, thus Child of Hotevilla.

Balukai Mesa, Arizona: Baalók'aa'í

baa - *near it, alongside it* • lók'aa' - *reeds*

Reeds near it or alongside it. The mesa, west of Salina (Tsé Láni), is 20 miles in
length from north to south, and is separated from Black Mesa (Dziłijiin) on the
north by Burnt Corn Wash (Naadą́ą́' Diílid).

Bear's Ears, Utah: Shashjaa'

shash - *bear* • jaa' - *ear(s)*

Literally bear's ears. This formation near Bluff, Utah has the appearance, from
a distance, of the ears of a bear.

Bear Springs, Arizona: Shash Bitoo'

shash - *bear* • bi - *its* • too' - *spring, water*

Bear water. These springs are located about 3 miles north of Steamboat Canyon
(Tóyéé'). There are Anasazi ruins on the ridge above the springs. This Navajo name
is also given to Fort Wingate, New Mexico.

Beautiful Mountain, Arizona: Dziłk'i Hózhónii

dził - *mountain* • k'i - *on, upon, on top* • hózhǫ - *to become beautiful,
peaceful* • (n)ii - *the place, the one*

The mountain top that is beautiful. This mountain spur runs northeastward from
the main trunk of the Tunicha (Tóntsaa) range. Its elevation is 8,340 feet.

Beclabito, Arizona: Bitł'ááh Bito'

bi - *his, her, its* • tł'ááh - *underside, bottom* • bito' - *its water or spring*

A spring underneath. The location is in northeastern Arizona, on the slopes of
the Carrizo Mountains (Dził Náhooziłii).

Bekithatso Lake, Arizona: Be'ek'id Hatsoh

be'ek'id - *lake* • ha - *area, space* • tsoh - *large, big*

A lake of large area. This Navajo stock-watering lake is between Chinle (Ch'ínílį)
and Balukai Mesa (Baalók'aa'í).

Bennett Peak, New Mexico: Tsé Naajiin

tsé - *stone, rock* • naa - *downward, descending* • jiin (jin) - *black*

Descending black rock. Bennett Peak, a volcanic plug, is 65 miles north of Gallup
(Na'nízhoozhí) and immediately to the west of Highway 666. It is also called
Tsézhin Íí'áhí (black rock projecting upward). *Tsé Naajiin* is also the Navajo name
for Cabezon Butte, north of Mount Taylor (Tsoodził), New Mexico.

Betatakin, Arizona: Bitát'ahkin

bitát'ah - *a rock ledge, rock ledges* • kin - *house(s), building(s)*

A house on a rock ledge, or houses on rock ledges. The name refers to the Anasazi
ruins in Betatakin National Monument, north of Marsh Pass (Bitát'ah Dzígai or
Tsé Yík'áán).

4

Betatakin, Arizona: Bitát'ahkin

Bidahochee, Arizona: Bidahóóchii'

bidah - *down, downward* • hó(ó) - *space, area* • chii' - *the color of red ochre*

A red area coming down, extending downward. This spring and trading post is located about 19 miles southwest of Greasewood (Díwózhii Bii' Tó). The name may refer to a rock slide on a hill near the trading post.

Big Oak, Arizona: Tséch'iltsoh

tsé - *rock, stone* • ch'il - *plant* • tséch'il - *rock plant, oak* • tsoh - *big, large*

Literally big rock plant, big oak. Big Oak is a few miles northwest of Rock Point (Tsé Ntsaa Deez'áhí).

Big Mountain, Arizona: Dził Ntsaa

dził - *mountain* • ntsaa - *big, large*

A mountain that is big. This large mountainous ridge runs north and south on the southwestern flanks of Black Mesa (Dziłíjiin), some 55 miles south of Kayenta (Tó Dínéeshzhee')

Bird Spring, Arizona: Tsídiito'í

tsidii - *bird* • to' - *water, spring* • í - *the place*

The place where birds come for water. Bird Spring is about 10 miles southeast of Leupp (Tsiizizii), Arizona.

Bisti, New Mexico: Bistahí
bis - *clay, adobe, bank, arroyo* • tah - *among* • í - *the place*

The place among the clay or adobe formations. This eroded, multi-form landscape is located in the desert some 30 miles south of Farmington (Tóta').

Bisti, New Mexico: Bistah

Bitani Tsosie Wash, New Mexico: K'ai' Naashchii' Bikooh
k'ai' - *willow tree* • naashchii' - *a serpentine or meandering red line* • bikooh - *canyon, arroyo, wash*

A meandering red willow wash. The arroyo in Chaco Canyon forms the central branch of the Escavada Wash (Gah Adádí), 3 miles north of Pueblo Bonito (Tsé Bíyah Anii'áhí). It is named after Slim Bitani, a wealthy Navajo stock owner.

Black Mesa, Arizona: Dziłíjiin
dził - *mountain* • (y)íjiin - *it is black*

The mountain is black, black mountain. This vast mesa extends from the Rough Rock (Tsé Ch'izhí) area to the Hopi country (Ayahkinii) to the southwest. It has been exploited for its huge coal deposits.

Black Mountain Sitting Up, Arizona: Dził Dahshzhinii
dził - *mountain* • dah - *up at an elevation* • shzhin (łizhin) - *black* • ii - *the one*

A black mountain sitting up at an elevation, also black spot mountain. The mountain is situated at the extreme northern end of Big Mountain (Dził Ntsaa) on the southwestern slopes of Black Mesa (Dziłíjiin).

Black Mountain Store, Arizona: Tók'i Hazbi̜'í

tó - *water* • k'i - *on it, over it* • hazbi̜' - *a hogan is built* • í - *the place*

A place where a shelter has been built over water, in this case a well. This location is about 25 miles west of Chinle (Ch'ínílí̜).

Black Pinnacle , Arizona: Shash Dits'iní

shash - *bear* • dits'in - *to become hard, to be seasoned* • í - *the place*

A tough old bear. The origin of this name is unknown. This site is 12 miles southeast of Lukachukai (Lók'a'ch' égai, Lók'a'jígai). A rough volcanic rim above pine and pinyon woods, this height offers splendid views to the west and south. It was selected by the Indian Forest Service in 1937 as a lookout.

Black Point, Arizona: Tsézhin Deez'áhí

tsé - *rock* • zhin - *black* • tsézhin - *black rock, lava* • deez'á - *it extends as a long ridge, bluff, or mountain* • (h)í - *the one*

Black rock or lava extending as a long ridge. This lava mass is an adjunct to San Francisco Peak (Dook'o'oosłíid) and its surrounding flanks. A volcanic field, it extends toward the Little Colorado River, 25 miles upstream from Cameron (Na'ní'á Hayázhí). Tradition has it that the Navajos used this area as a stopping place on their migration to Navajo Mountain (Naatsis'áán).

Black Rock, Arizona: Chézhiní

ché - *rock* • zhin • í - *the one*

Literally a black rock. The site of this volcanic formation is 2 miles south of Fort Defiance (Tséhootsooí). The rock is also called Tł'iishtsoh Baghan (Big Snake's House) in the Navajo Windway Ceremony (Níłch'iji). Big Snake supposedly lives within Chézhiní. Chézhiní, or Tsézhiní, is the name for many such volcanic plugs or dykes in Navajoland (Diné Bikéyah). One notable example is the large outcropping between Canyon de Chelly (Tséyi') and Canyon del Muerto (Ane'é Tséyi').

Black Rock, New Mexico: Tsézhi̜i̜h Deezlí̜

tsé - *rock* • zhi̜i̜h - *into black rock* (zhin - *black*, i̜i̜h - *into*) • deezlí̜ - *it starts to flow, it flows*

It flows into black rock. The reference is to the stream flowing from the Zuni Mountains (Naasht'ézhí Dził) into Black Rock Lake near Zuni (Naasht'ézhí), where some of the rock is of volcanic origin.

Blanco, New Mexico: Taahóóteel

taa (taah) - *into the water, the river* • hó(ó) - *space, area* • teel - *broad, wide, flat*

A wide area extending down to or into the water. Blanco is a Spanish-American farming community 14 miles southeast of Aztec (Kinteel). The area is also known as Largo Canyon (Tsiíd Bii' Tó). This canyon is one of the principal contributaries to the San Juan River (Tooh, Tooh Bika̜'í, Nóóda'í Bitooh, Sá̜ Bitooh).

Blanco Canyon, New Mexico: T'iistah Diiteelí

t'iis - *cottonwood* • tah - *among* • diiteel - *it is wide, broad, spread out* • í - *the place*

Spread out among the cottonwoods. This broad and sandy canyon has cottonwoods at places along its banks. Its heading is at Lybrook (Tónáálíní), New Mexico and it joins Largo Canyon (Tsiíd Bii' Tó) 40 miles to the north at Salt Point (Áshi̜i̜h Náá'á).

Bloomfield, New Mexico: Naabi'ááni

naa (naa') - *enemy* • bi - *his, her, its* • a'áán - *cave* • i - *the place*

The place of the enemy's cave. The enemy referred to may have been the Ute or the Comanche. The small town at the site today is on the north bank of the San Juan River (Tooh, Tooh Bįką'i, Nóóda'i Bitooh, Sá Bitooh), nine miles southeast of Aztec (Kinteel).

Blue Canyon, Arizona: Bikooh Hodootł'izh

bikooh - *canyon, wash, arroyo* • ho - *space, area* • dootł'izh - *it is green or blue*

A canyon area that is of a greenish or bluish cast. There is one site with this name near Fort Defiance (Tséhootsooi) and another in the proximity of Kayenta (Tódínéeshzhee'). The latter forms the northern drainage on Black Mesa (Dziłijiin). The former is also called *Tsézhin Hodootł'izh* (blue or green lava area).

Blue House, New Mexico: Díwózhiishzhiin

díwózhii - *greasewood, chamizo (Atriplex sarcobatus)* • (sh)zhiin - *it is black*

Black greasewood. This ruin is located 6 miles east of Pueblo Bonito (Tsé Biyah Anii'áhí). It is also known as Turquoise House (Kin Dootł'izhí), as well as Wijiji, Vetege-Tchi, and Greasewood House.

Bluewater, New Mexico: T'iis Ntsaa Ch'ééłį

t'iis - *cottonwood tree(s)* • ntsaa - *it is large, big* • ch'ééłį - *it flows out horizontally*

The place where water flows out horizontally near large cottonwood trees. The reference here is to one of the streams flowing from the Zuni Mountains (Naasht'ézhí Dził) and feeding Bluewater Lake.

Bodoway, Arizona: Ba'adíwei

Ba'adíwei is the Navajo pronunciation of the name of a Paiute chief for whom the site was named. It is on the west side of Echo Cliffs at Marble Canyon.

Bonito Canyon, Arizona: Tséhootsooi Ch'inílį

tsé - *rock* • hootso - *meadow* • i - *the place* • ch'i - *out, out from* nílí - *it flows*

It flows out from the place where there is a rock meadow. This name refers to the mouth of Bonito Canyon, behind Fort Defiance (Tséhootsooi).

Borrego Pass, New Mexico: Dibé Yázhí Habitiin

dibé - *sheep* • yázhí - *little,small* • ha - *out, outward* • bi - *its, their* (a)tiin - *track(s), road, path*

Little sheep (lamb) tracks coming out. This location is about 11 miles southeast of Crownpoint (T'iists'óózi, T'iists'óóz Ńdeeshgizh).

Bosque Redondo, (Fort Sumner), New Mexico: Hwéeldi

This name is probably the Navajo approximation of the Spanish word *fuerte* (fort), or a possible corruption of Navajo *awáalyadi* (at the prison). Bosque Redondo, now Fort Sumner, was the site of the internment of the Navajos after the Long March or Long Walk of 1863-64. The old Navajos called the place *T'iis Názbąs* (cottonwoods in a circle). Hwéeldi is in eastern New Mexico on U.S. Highway 60.

Box-S Ranch, New Mexico: **Kin Na'ní'á**
kin - *house* • na'ní'á - *a bridge*
Literally a bridged house. The provenience of this name is obscure. This abandoned ranch is situated some 3 miles southeast of Nutria (Tsé Dijįhí).

Bread Springs, New Mexico: **Bááh Háálį**
bááh - *bread* • háálį - *it flows up and out*
Bread flows up and out. The name is of unknown origin. This community is in the rolling foothills of the Zuni Mountains (Naasht'ézhí Dził) about 20 miles south of Gallup.

Buell Park, New Mexico: **Ni' Hooldzis**
ni' - *earth* • hoo - *area, space* • (l)dzis - *it is hollowed out, furrowed, basin shaped*
Earth hollowed out or basin shaped. This area is a basin or bowl of open land between Fort Defiance (Tséhootsooí) and Sawmill (Ni'iijíhí), to the north. Buell Park is also called *Ni' Haldzis*, a term having the same meaning given above.

Bunched Feathers, Arizona: **T'á'nááséél**
t'á' - *feathers* • nááséél - *a crowd is moving back*
A crowd of people is moving back with feathers. The name refers to a depiction in a petroglyph in Canyon de Chelly (Tséyi').

Burnham, New Mexico: **T'iistsoh Sikaad**
t'iis - *cottonwood tree* • tsoh - *big, large* • sikaad - *it stands spreading*
Big cottonwoods stand spread out. This site is about 60 miles northeast of Gallup (Na'nízhoozhí) in barren desert country near Chaco Canyon (Tsé Bíyah Anii'áhí).

Burnt Corn, Arizona: **Naadą́ą́' Díílid**
naadą́ą́' - *corn* (naa' - *enemy;* dą́ą́' - *food*) • díílid - *it is burnt*
Corn that is burnt. This wash and Anasazi ruin are in the Pinon (Be'ek'id Baa Ahoodzání) area.

Cabezón Butte, New Mexico: **Tsé Naajiin**
tsé - *rock* • naa - *downward* • jiin (jin) - *it is black*
Black rock coming downward. This prominent volcanic plug is about 12 miles northeast of Mount Taylor (Tsoodził) and some 40 miles northwest of Albuquerque (Bee'eldíildahsinil). The former village of Cabezón nearby was rendered as *Gawasóón* by the Navajos. The word *cabezón* means *big head* in Spanish, and the butte is identified in Navajo mythology as the head of Yé'iitsoh (see Anzac, New Mexico). *Tsé Naajiin* is also the Navajo name for Bennett Peak, New Mexico.

Cache Mountain, New Mexico: **Yisdá Dziil**
yisdá - *refuge, safety, rescue* • dziil - *mountain*
A mountain where there is safety, refuge mountain. Cache Mountain is near La Ventana, in northwestern New Mexico.

Cameron, Arizona: **Na'ní'á Hayázhí**
na'ní'á - *something rigid extends across, a bridge* • ha - *area, space*
yázhí - *small*

A small span or bridge. This community is situated on the south bank of the Little Colorado Gorge. The bridge, known as Government Bridge, was built in 1911, the same year of the founding of the community. Cameron is about 55 miles north of Flagstaff (Kin Łání).

Cabezón Butte, New Mexico: Tsé Naajíí

Cañoncito, New Mexico: Tó Hajiileehé

tó - *water* • hajiileeh - *they pull them up one after another suspended at the end of a rope or cord* (in this case, buckets) • é (í) - *the place*

The place where they pull them up one after another. The allusion here is to a well from which water is drawn up by a bucket, or buckets, on a rope. Cañoncito, a Navajo community and day school, is about 27 miles east of Laguna (Tó Łání) and north of U.S Highway I-40.

Canyon de Chelly, Arizona: Tséyi'

tsé - *rock(s)* • yi' - *within,inside*

Within the rocks. The term refers to any canyon in Navajo. The name *Chelly* is evidently of Spanish origin, an attempt to render the Navajo word *Tséyi'*. The spelling *Chelly* is pronounced *shay*. This spectacular canyon runs from Chinle (Ch'ínílí) northeastward to the Tsaile (Tsééhílí) and Wheatfields (Tó Dzis'á) areas.

Canyon del Muerto, Arizona: Ane'é Tséyi'

ane' - *behind it* • é (í) - *the one, the place* • tsé - *rock(s)* • yi' - *within it or them* • tséyi' - *a canyon*

The canyon behind. Canyon del Muerto enters Canyon de Chelly (Tséyi') 4 or 5 miles northeast of Chinle (Ch'inilį). Colonel Chacon and his troops in 1805 reputedly massacred some 70 Navajo women and children in Canyon del Muerto (Sp. Canyon of Death). Chacon headed a contingent of Spanish and Zunis.

Canyon del Muerto, Arizona: Ane'é Tséyi'

Canyon Diablo, Arizona: Kin Łigaai
kin - *house, building* • łigai - *it is white* • i - *the one*

Literally a white house. This name is reported to refer to the old Voltz Trading Post on the Santa Fe Railroad. The canyon enters the Little Colorado River (Tółchi'ikooh) a mile or so northwest of Leupp (Tsiizizii). *Kin Łigaai* is also the Navajo name for Baca, San Juan Pueblo, and Sandia Pueblo, all in New Mexico, and for Navajo Springs and Moenave in Arizona.

Carrizo Mountains, Arizona: Dził Náhooziłii
dził - *mountain(s)* • náhooził - *it gropes, whirls* • ii - *the one*

Groping or whirling mountain. This peculiar name may refer to the tortuous and deep black-rock canyons that cut into the mountain on all of its flanks. A satellite photograph reveals the mountain to be nearly circular. The Carrizos form the last segment, separated by the Red Rock (Tsé Lichíí' Dah Azkání) area, of the Chuska (Ch'óshgai) and Lukachukai (Lók'a'ch'égai) Mountain complex. Dził Náhooziłii is situated in the extreme northeastern corner of Arizona.

Carson, New Mexico: Hanáádlį
ha - *up, out* • náá - *again, another* • (d)lį - *it flows*

It flows up or out again. This location is on the east side of the Gallegos Wash (Teeł Sikaad), 30 miles south of Farmington (Tóta').

Casa Rinconada, New Mexico: Kin Názbąs
kin - *house* • názbąs - *it is circular*

Literally a circular house. The name refers to the ruin of an enormous kiva in Chaco Canyon (Tsé Bíyah Anii'áhí). It is situated on a small knoll about ¼ mile south of Pueblo Bonito. This ceremonial kiva has an inside diameter of 62 feet.

Casa San Martin, Gallup, New Mexico: Atoo' Ditsxizi
atoo' - *soup, stew* • ditsxiz - *it shakes, trembles* • i - *the place*

The place where soup shakes. Shaky soup. Casa San Martin is a soup kitchen and refuge in Gallup (Na'nízhoozhí). The name describes the soup in the trembling hands of a heavy drinker the morning after.

Cebolleta, New Mexico: Tł'ohchin
tł'oh - *grass* • chin - *smell, odour* • tł'ohchin - *onion(s)*

Onion, or onions. The legume referred to is the wild onion (*Allium cernuum*). This old New Mexican farming village is 13 miles north of Laguna Pueblo (Tó Łání) on the eastern slope of the Cebolleta Mountains. The word *cebolleta* (cebollita) is a Spanish diminuitive meaning *small onion*.

Cedar Hills Grocery and Liquor, Gallup New Mexico: Hajíízíni
hajíízį - *standing up halfway (out of an arroyo, hole, or depresssion)* • (n)i - *the place*

The place where people stand up halfway out of the arroyo. This name refers to the spot in the arroyo behind the store where a group will stand up, gopher-like, looking and waiting for their companion to bring them liquor from the establishment.

Cedar Ridge, Arizona: Yaaniilk'id
yaa - *down, downward* • niilk'id - *a hill runs to a point where it stops*

A downward sloping hill that comes to a stop. This sandstone ridge lies 40 miles north of Cameron (Na'ní'á Hayázhi). The ridge, high and shear, is thickly populated with pinyon and juniper trees on its eastern side. It is said to have been a camping ground for traveling bands of Paiutes.

Cedar Springs, Arizona: K'iishzhinii
k'iish - *alder, alders* • zhin - *black* • ii - *the place*

The place of black alders, or ironwood (*Carpinus americana*). The springs are situated some 30 miles north of Winslow (Béésh Sinil) on the road to the Hopi villages (Ayahkinii). Part of this region was added to the Navajo reservation between 1910 and 1929.

Cedar Standing, Arizona: Gad Íí'áhí
gad - *cedar tree, juniper* • íí'á - *it stands, projects upward* • (h)i - *the place*

The place where cedar stands, cedar standing. Only the stumps of two cedar trees are said to be left at this site some 30 miles northeast of Oraibi (Oozéí) and 65 miles southwest of the rim of Black Mesa (Dziłíjiin).

Chaco Canyon, New Mexico: Tsé Bíyah Anii'áhí
tsé - *rock* • bíyah - *under it* • anii'á - *something extends along* • (h)i - *the place*

The place where something extends along under the rock. The Anasazi people of Chaco Canyon built a masonry support under a large boulder which threatened to break off of the cliff above the pueblo. The huge rock fell in 1941. Chaco Canyon, one of the grandest of the Anasazi ruins, lies some 30 miles northeast of Crownpoint (T'iists'óóz Ńdeeshgizh).

Chama, New Mexico: Ts'i'mah

Ts'i'mah is the Navajo version of a Tewa word meaning a *wrestling place*. The location is in extreme north-central New Mexico, south of the Chama mountains, which the Navajos call *Ts'i'mah Dziil*. North of these mountains lie the San Juans (Dibé Ntsaa) of Colorado, with peaks over 13,000 feet.

Chambers, Arizona: Ch'ilzhóó'

ch'il - *plant, weed, bush, shrub* • zhóó' - *a stem connoting sweeping or brushing*

The plant with which one can sweep or brush, in this case silver sagebrush or sand sage *(Artemesia filifolia)*. This location is 49 miles east of Holbrook (T'iisyaakin). The site was named for a railroader named Chambers. It is less than 2 miles east of Taylor Springs (Asdzání Taah Yíyá).

Charley Day Spring, Arizona: Séí Haha'eeł

séí - *sand* • ha - *up and out* • ha(ho) - *space, area* • 'eeł - *it floats*

Sand floats up and out. This spring near Tuba City (Tónaneesdizi) was named for Charley Day, a Navajo scout in the Apache campaign of 1885. He had his home *(hooghan)* at this site. Excavations near this location revealed extinct species of horse, bison, elephants, and camels, as well as traces of early man.

Cheechilgeeto, New Mexico: Chéch'iltah

ché (tsé) - *rock* • ch'il - *plant* • chéch'il - *rock plant, i.e., oak tree* • tah - *among*

Among the oak trees. A trading post and a government day school are situated at this site about 30 miles southwest of Gallup (Na'nízhoozhí).

Chetro Kettle, New Mexico: Tsé Bidádi'ni'áni

tsé - *rock* • bidádi' - *blocking it* • ni'á - *solid objects lie in a row or line* • (n)i - *the one*

Rock that is plugged or sealed up. The name alludes to a series of sealed concavities or niches in the wall of this kiva. Chetro Kettle, a major ruin in Chaco Canyon (Tsé Bíyah Anii'áhí), is about ½ mile east of Pueblo Bonito.

Chilchinbito, Arizona: Chiiłchin Bii' Tó, Tsiiłchin Bii' Tó

chiiłchin, tsiiłchin - *odorous wood, sumac (Rhus canadensis)* • bii' - *in it, within it* • tó - *water*

Water within (among) the sumac trees. This location is 25 miles south of Kayenta (Tó Dínéeshzhee'), beneath the northeastern rim of Black Mountain (Dziłijiin). Navajo women are said to have woven basketry from the sumac growing near and around the spring.

China Springs, New Mexico: K'aałáni

kaa' - *reeds, arrows* • łáni - *many*

Many reeds. The reference is to the reeds growing in a large spring-formed pond at the site. This location is about 2 miles north of Gamerco (Łigaiyaa'áhí). The Navajos reportedly attacked a group of Kit Carson's troops here in 1863, but evidently bullets, rather than arrows, were used.

Chinle, Arizona: Ch'ínílį̇́

ch'í - *out, outward* • nílį̇́ - *it flows*

The place where it flows out. The name refers to the stream that flows down from the Chuska Mountains (Ch'óshgai) through Canyon de Chelly (Tséyi') and debouches at Chinle. Chinle is some 65 miles northwest of Window Rock (Tségháhoodzání).

Churchrock, New Mexico: Kinłitsosinil

kin - *house, building, store* • łitso - *it is yellow, they are yellow* • sinil - *they are in position*

Yellow houses in position. This small village near Gallup is named for the khaki-colored government buildings constructed there during World War II. This housing was originally painted yellow. The Navajo name for Church Rock Spires, north of the community, is *Tsé Íí'áhí* (standing rock(s)).

Churchrock Spires, New Mexico: Tsé Íí'áhí

tsé - *rock* • íí'á - *it stands, projects upward* • í - *the one*

Standing rock. The name refers to the prominent twin spires of rock east of Gallup (Na'nízhoozhí) and just north of the village of Churchrock (Kinłitsosinil). This name is also given to other distinctive projections of stone in Navajo country (Diné Bikéyah). Notable are Standing Rock, New Mexico, near Coyote Canyon (Mą'ii Tééh Yítlizhí), and Four Corners, where the states of Arizona, Colorado, New Mexico, and Utah meet.

Chuska Pass, New Mexico: Tsé Bii' Naayolí

tsé - *rock* • bii' - *within it* • naayol - *the wind blows about* • í - *the place*

The place where the wind blows around within the rocks. The pass is located in the southern reaches of the Chuska Mountains (Ch'óshgai). One fork of the road goes to Tohatchi (Tóhaach'i'), the other to Mexican Springs (Naakaii Bito').

Chuska Peak, New Mexico: Ch'óshgai

ch'ó - *spruce (Pseudotsuga mucronata)* • (sh)gai - *white, it is white*

White spruce. This mountain peak north of Gallup (Na'nízhoozhí) at one time had stands of spruce, fir and ponderosa. The peak, just northwest of Tohatchi (Tóhaach'i'), is clearly visible from Gallup, some 25 miles to the south.

Coalmine Canyon, Arizona: Honooji

honooji - *to be rough, rugged, serrated, jagged*

A rugged, jagged area. This name alludes to the Bryce Canyon type of erosion. The site is about 17 miles southeast of Tuba City (Tónaneesdizí).

Coalmine Pass, Arizona: Tséteeł Naagaii

tsé - *rock or rocks* • teeł - *wide, broad* • naa - *descending, coming down* • gai - *white* • í - *the one*

Wide rock coming down white. This pass is about 15 miles southwest of Chuska Peak (Ch'óshgai). The western opening of the pass is 6 miles east of Fort Defiance (Tséhootsooí) and the eastern entrance is some 4 miles west of Mexican Springs (Naakaii Bito').

14

Coconino Point and Plateau, Arizona: Dził Libái
dził - *mountain* • libá - *it is gray* • i - *the one*
The mountain that is gray, gray mountain. The plateau is situated about 8 miles southwest of Cameron (Na'ni'á Hayázhí). It is bounded on the north by the Little Colorado River (Tółchi'ikooh).

Cold Spring, Arizona: Tó Sik'az Háálį
tó - *water* • sik'az - *it is cold* • háálį - *it flows up and out*
Cold water flows up and out. The spring is some 15 miles southeast of Canyon de Chelly (Tséyi') and 2 miles north of Piney Hill tower.

Concho, Arizona: Tóts'ózí
tó - *water* • ts'ózí - *it is slim, narrow*
Slim water. The community of Concho is on this narrow creek situated about 15 miles southwest of St. Johns (Tsézhin Deez'áhí, Chézhin Deez'áhí).

Continental Divide, New Mexico: Ahideelk'id
ahi - *to come together, converge* • deelk'id - *hills in a line*
Lines of hills come together. This site on the Continental Divide is about 8 miles west of Thoreau (Dlǫ'áyázhi) on U.S. Highway I-40.

Coolidge, New Mexico: Chishi Nééz
Chishi - *Chiricahua Apache* • nééz - *tall*
Tall Chiricahua Apache. The origin of this Navajo appelation is obscure. The location is 20 miles east of Gallup (Na'nízhoozhí) on U.S. Highway I-40. The community was once the shipping center for Fort Wingate (Shash Bitoo').

Coppermine, Arizona: Tsinaabąąs Habitiin
tsinaabąąs - *wagon* (tsin - *wood;* naabąąs - *it rolls about*) • ha - *up and out* • bi- *its* • (a)tiin - *road, trail*
Wagon road up and out. The mine was situated 25 miles north of The Gap, for which this trail was named. Copper was located here as early as the 1880's.

Cornfields, Arizona: K'iiłtsoiitah
k'iiłtsoii - *rabbit bush (Chrysothamus graveolens)* • tah - *among*
Among the rabbit bush. This Bureau of Indian Affairs day school is about 10 miles southwest of Ganado (Lók'aahnteel).

Cortez, Colorado: Tséyaatóhí
tsé - *rock* • yaa - *under, beneath* • tó - *water* • (h)i - *the place*
The place where there is water under the (a) rock. This town in southwestern Colorado is the western entry point to Mesa Verde National Park (Gad Deelzhah, Nóóda'i Dził).

Cottonwood Pass, New Mexico: Béésh Łichii'ii Bigiizh
béésh - *metal* • łichii' - *it is red* • ii - *the one* • bi - *its* • giizh - *gap, pass, cut*
Red metal (copper) pass. The name refers to the metallic rock formations in the gap. It was named Washington Pass after Lieutenant Colonel John Washington, military governor of New Mexico, who passed through the pass during an expedition against the Navajos in 1849. Since 1992 it has been officially designated as Narbona Pass, in honor of the 19th century Navajo chieftain who lived in the region.

Cottonwood Pass, New Mexico: Béésh Lichíi'ii Bigiiz

Cottonwood Tank, Arizona: T'iis Sitáni
t'iis - *cottonwood tree(s)* • sitá - *it is lying* • (n)í - *the place*

The place where the cottonwood is lying. This holding basin and watering location for the Navajos is 3 miles south of The Gap (Tsinaabąąs Habitiin) and about 1 mile east of U.S. Highway 89.

Counselors, New Mexico: Bilagáana Nééz
bilágaana - *white man* • nééz - *tall*

Tall white man. The site is 28 miles west of Cuba (Na'azísí To'í), New Mexico and west of the Continental Divide on New Mexico Highway 55. The tall white man was James Counselor, a former trader.

Cove, Arizona: K'aabizhii, K'aabizhiistł'ah
k'aabizhii - *a small hooked-spine cactus* • (s)tł'ah (nástł'ah) - *a corner*

A corner of small hooked-spine cactus. This expansive cove lies in the red sandstone area that articulates the Lukachukai (Lók'a'ch'égai) and Carrizo Mountains (Dził Náhoozilii). It is about 15 miles northeast of Round Rock (Tsé Nikání). It is said to be an old rendevous and hiding spot of the Navajos.

The Cowboy Bar, Gallup New Mexico: Ch'izhnílnįįhí
ch'i - *out, outward* • (zh)nílnįįh - *someone peers, looks* • í - *the place*

The place where someone peers out. The bar is so named by the Navajo because of the drive-up window where a clerk peers out to take a customer's order.

16

Coyote Canyon, New Mexico: Mąʼii Tééh Yitłizhi
mąʼii - *coyote* • tééh - *deep water* • yítłizh - *he, she fell in* • i - *the place*
The place where the coyote fell into deep water. This savagely eroded canyon is immediately to the north of Mesa de los Lobos (Dził) and about 10 miles east of Mexican Springs (Naakaii Bitoʼ).

Crooked Oak, New Mexico: Tséchʼil Ńdeezwod
tsé - *rock* • chʼil - *plant* • tséchʼil - *rock plant, i.e., oak* • ńdeezwod - *crooked*
Literally crooked or deformed oak. This canyon or wash is north of Windy Canyon (Tsé Biiʼ Naayolí) and empties into Todilto (Todildǫʼ) Wash just east of Navajo (Niʼiijíhí), New Mexico.

Cross Canyon, Arizona: Béésh Dichʼizhii
béésh - *flintstone, metal, iron* • dichʼizh - *it is rough* • ii - *the one*
Rough flintstone. The site of an old trading post, the canyon was a well-traveled crossing point for the Navajos of the area.

Cross Canyon Trail, Arizona: Ałnaashii Haʼatiin
ałnaashii - *opposite one another, on opposite sides* • ha - *up , upward* • atiin - *a trail or road, trails or roads*
A trail that goes up on opposite sides. This trail is, or was, in use by Navajos crossing between Canyon del Muerto (Aneʼé Tséyiʼ) and Canyon de Chelly (Tséyiʼ). It is near Fir Line Trail (Chʼódááʼ Haaztʼiʼ).

Crossing of the Fathers, Arizona: Tódááʼ Nʼdeetiin
tó - *water* • dááʼ - *edge* • nʼdeetiin - *a trail or road across*
A trail across at the edge of the water. The missionary Fathers Dominguez and Escalante are said to have forded this crossing in 1776. It is located on the Colorado River about 14 miles up from the opening of Navajo Canyon (Tsékooh Niitsįʼii).

Crownpoint, New Mexico: Tʼiistsʼóóz Ńdeeshgizh
tʼiis - *cottonwood* • tsʼóóz - *slender, slim* • ńdeeshgizh - *it is cut open, or gapped*
Slender cottonwood gap. Crownpoint is located about 30 miles northeast of Thoreau (Dlǫ́ʼáyázhí) and 3 miles north of Hosta Butte Mesa (Akʼidah Nástʼání, Akʼiih Nástʼání). The community is also known simply as Tʼiistsʼóózí (slender cottonwoods place).

Crystal, New Mexico: Tóniłtsʼílí
tó - *water* • niłtsʼilí - *it sparkles, is crystalline*
Sparkling water. The community is on the west side of the Tunicha (Tóntsaa) range. The stream originates near Washington Pass (Béésh Łichííʼii Bigiizh) and flows through Crystal, which is about 10 miles northeast of Red Lake (Beʼekʼid Halchííʼ).

Cuba, New Mexico: Naʼazísí Toʼí
naʼazísí - *gopher* • tó - *water, spring* • i - *the place*
Gopher spring. Cuba, a Spanish-American community, is situated about 70 miles northwest of Albuquerque (Beeʼeldííldahsinil) on New Mexico Highway 55. Its Navajo name alludes to a Navajo chief named *Hastiin Naʼazísí* (Mr. Gopher), whose spring abounded in gophers.

17

Cubero, New Mexico: Tsék'iz Tóhí

tsé - *rock* • k'iz - *crevice* • tó - *water* • (h)í - *the place*

The place where there is water in a crevice. This old 18th century town is in the mesa area south of Mount Taylor (Tsoodził). It was a trading center for the Navajos and a Spanish military outpost.

Cudai, New Mexico: Gad Íí'áí

gad - *juniper or cedar tree* • íí'á - *it sticks up, projects upward* • í - *the place*

The place where the juniper tree sticks up. This community and irrigated farming area is on the south side of the San Juan River (Tooh, Tooh Biką'í, Nóóda'í Bitooh, Są Bitooh) about 5 miles west of the community of Shiprock (Naat'áanii Nééz, Toohdi).

Dalton's Pass, New Mexico: Nihodeeshgiizh

niho - *space extending downward* • deeshgiizh - *a gap or pass*

The gap that descends or goes downward. This pass descends from Mariano Lake (Be'ek'id Hóteel) at the northern end of La Mesa de los Lobos (Dził) into the Standing Rock (Tsé Íí'áhí) area. The pass served as a conduit for the old wagon and horse trail that was the main route to the San Juan River (Tooh, Tooh Biką'í, Nóóda'í Bitooh, Są Bitooh).

Deer Springs, Arizona: Biįh Bito'

biįh - *deer* • bi - *its* • to' - *water, spring*

Deer water, deer spring. Deer Springs is just northeast of the new dam at Blue Canyon (Bikooh Hodootl'izh), near Fort Defiance (Tséhootsooí).

Defiance Station, New Mexico: Tsé Ńdeeshgiizh

tsé - *rock* • ńdeeshgiizh - *a gap, or cut*

A gap in the rock. A former trading post was situated at this spot 6 miles west of Gallup (Na'nízhoozhí) near Twin Buttes (Chézhin). The Navajo name refers to a formidable gap in a nearby mesa.

Dennihotso, Arizona: Deinihootso

dei - *up, upward* • niho(o) - *space or area* • tso - *yellow, becoming yellow*

A yellow or yellowish area, or meadow, extending upward. This sandy agricultural valley is 27 miles east of Kayenta (Tó Díneeshzhee') and about 10 miles southwest of Mexican Water (Naakaii Tó, Naakaii Tó Hadayiiznilí).

Dilcon, Arizona: Tsézhin Dilkǫǫh

tsé - *rock* • zhin - *black* • dilkǫǫh - *it is smooth*

Smooth black rock, or smooth lava. The name alludes to the butte southwest of the community. Dilcon is about 35 miles northeast of Winslow (Béésh Sinil).

Dinnebito, Arizona: Diné Bito'

diné - *Navajo, person, man* • bi - *his, her, its* • to' - *water, spring*

Navajo Spring. This location is some 15 miles south of Oraibi (Oozéí) in the barren Dinnebito Wash, which heads on Black Mesa (Dziłíjiin) and flows southwestward into the Hopi (Ayahkinii) reservation.

Dinnebito Dam, Arizona: Tsé De Nínít'i'í
tsé - *rock* • de - *up, upward* • nínít'i' - *it ends* • í - *the place*
The place where the rock extends upward and ends. The U.S Indian Service built a concrete diversion dam on the Dinnebito Wash at this site near Dinnebito (Diné Bito') in 1937.

Dinosaur Canyon, Arizona: Tsé Ndoolzhaai
tsé - *rock* • ndoolzha - *it extends downward in jagged form* • í - *the place*
Jagged rock descending. The canyon is 14 miles southeast of Cameron (Na'ní'á Hayázhí). Many footprints of three-toed dinosaurs are preserved in white sandstone here. The Navajos call these tracks *tsídiinabitiin* (bird tracks).

Doney Mountain, Arizona: Dził Łichíí'
dził - *mountain* • łichíí' - *it is red*
Red mountain. This volcanic cone is 4 miles northwest of Wupatki Ruin (Anaasází Bikin), which is in Wupatki National Monument, 40 miles north of Flagstaff (Kin Łání).

Dry Farm Wash, Arizona: Dibáá' Dá'ák'eh
dibáá' - *thirst* • dá'ák'eh - *field*
Thirst field. The site is about 10 miles to the west of Teec Nos Pos (T'iis Názbas), in the Four Corners (Tsé Íí'áhí) area.

Dulce, New Mexico: Beehai Kééhat'į
bee - *with it, by means of it* • hai - *winter* • kééhat'į - *he, she, it lives, dwells* • Beehai - *Jicarilla Apache*
Where the Jicarilla Apache live. Dulce is on the northern part of the Jicarilla Apache reservation. This is a mountainous area 17 miles west of Chama (Ts'í'mah).

Durango, Colorado: Kin Łání
kin - *house or houses, buildings* • łání - *many*
Many houses. Durango, in southern Colorado, is the gateway to the La Plata Mountains (Dibé Ntsaa). It is about 60 miles northeast of Farmington (Tóta'), New Mexico. *Kin Łání* is also the name for Flagstaff, Arizona.

Eagle Crag, Arizona: Tséłigai Dah Azkání
tsé - *rock* • łigai - *it is white* • dah - *up at an elevation* • azką - *flat-topped* • dah azką - *mesa* • (n)í - *the one, the place*
Flat-topped white rock up at an elevation. A white mesa. A sandstone crag about 4 miles west of Steamboat Canyon (Tóyéé'), this old nesting place for eagles contains a 14th century Anasazi ruin.

El Capitan, Arizona: Aghaałą́
aghaa' - *wool, fur* • łą - *much*
Much wool. See *Agathla Peak, Arizona.*

El Morro, New Mexico: Tsék'i Na'asdzooí
tsé - *rock* • k'i - *upon* • na'asdzo - *there is marking or writing* • í - *the place, the one*

El Morro, New Mexico: Tsék'i Na'asdzo(

The rock upon which there is writing. This massive rock is also known as *Tséiikiin* (the rock upon which there is sustenance). Its other English name is Inscription Rock. A national monument since 1906, El Morro is 15 miles east of Ramah (Tł'ohchiní) and 43 miles south of Grants (Natooh Sik'ai'í). The Spaniards, who named the rock *El Morro* (the bluff, promontory, headland), carved over 50 inscriptions on it, the earliest being that of Don Juan de Oñate in 1605. There are also numerous Anasazi petroglyphs on the formation. A deep, shady pool graces the east side of the rock and there are Anasazi ruins on the top.

Escavada Wash, New Mexico: Gah Adádí
gah - *rabbit* • adádí - *trap or ambush*

Rabbit ambush. A place where a hunter can ambush game. This spot is in one of the washes in the Chaco Canyon (Tsé Bíyah Anii'áhí) complex, 60 miles north of Thoreau (Dlǫ́'áyázhí), New Mexico.

Farmington, New Mexico: Tóta'
tó - *water* • ta' - *between*

Between the waters or rivers. The rivers referred to are the San Juan (Tooh, Tooh Bika'í, Nóóda'í Bitooh, Sǫ Bitooh) and the Animas, both flowing from the La Plata Mountains (Dibé Ntsaa) in Colorado.

Fir Line Trail, Arizona: Ch'ódáá' Haazt'i'
ch'ó - *fir trees* • dáá' - *edge or brink* • haazt'i' - *it extends up or out in a slender line*

Where the fir trees extend to the edge. This trail in Canyon del Muerto (Ane'é Tséyi') is near Twin or Cross Canyon Trail (Ałnaashii Ha'atiin).

Flagstaff, Arizona: Kin Łání
kin - house(s), building(s) • łání - many

Many houses. This town is on U.S I-40, in north-central Arizona. It is a stock and lumber shipping point as well as a wholesale center for Navajo and Hopi traders. Magnificent San Francisco Peak (Dook'o'oosłííd) looms nearby.

Flea Market, Gallup, New Mexico: Haazhdiilwo'ii
haa - up and out (a path or corridor) • diilwo' - running is done • ii - the place

The place where running or brisk walking is done up and out of corridors or paths. The flea market is held on the north side of Gallup (Na'nízhoozhí), not far south of Gamerco (Łigaiyaa'áhí), on Highway 666.

Fluted Rock, Arizona: Dził Dah Si'ání
dził - mountain • dah - up, up at an elevation • si'á - it sits • (n)í - the one, the place

The mountain that sits up at an elevation. This prominent mesa lies 18 miles northwest of Fort Defiance (Tséhootsooí) on the Defiance Plateau. It was evidently used as a heliographic signalling promontory during the Navajo campaign of 1863-4. Signals could reputedly be flashed as far away as Navajo Mountain (Naatsis'áán).

Forest Lake, Arizona: Tsinyi' Be'ek'id
tsin - tree(s), wood(s), forest • yi' - in, within • be'ek'id - lake

A lake within the trees or woods. The site is about 18 miles northwest of Pinon (Be'ek'id Baa Ahoodzání).

Fort Defiance, Arizona: Tséhootsooí
tsé - rock • hootso - meadow • í - the place

The place of the rock meadow. This name refers to the large, rocky meadow extending to the immediate west of the fort. Fort Defiance was the scene of many skirmishes between the Navajo and the U.S. military from 1856 to 1863.

Fort Sumner, New Mexico: Hwéeldi
The name Hwéeldi is probably a Navajo version of Spanish fuerte, meaning fort. See Bosque Redondo.

Fort Wingate, New Mexico: Shash Bitoo'
shash - bear • bi - its • too' - water, spring

Bear water, bear spring. The term originates from the spring at the site. This community lies at the northern base of the Zuni mountains, 18 miles east of Gallup (Na'nízhoozhí). The spring was a former watering place for bears inhabiting the mountains.

Four Corners, Arizona, Colorado, New Mexico, Utah: Tsé Íí'áhí
tsé - rock • íí'á - it stands up, sticks up • (h)í - the one

The rock that stands up, standing rock; or plural, standing rocks. This site marks the conjoining of the four states listed above. The Navajo name also refers to the community of Standing Rock, to the twin pinnacles east of Gallup (Na'nízhoozhí), and to other such projections of stone in Navajo country (Diné Bikéyah).

Fruitland, New Mexico: Bááh Díílid
bááh - *bread* • díílid - *it is burned*

Burned bread. It is said that Navajos were present at this site when Mormon settlers burned some bread. Fruitland, a small trading and farming community, is 10 miles west of Farmington (Tóta'). The Navajos also call the place *Niinah Nízaad* (long upgade) as well as *Doo Alk'aii* (no fat).

Fuzzy Mountain, New Mexico: Dził Dítł'oii
dził - *mountain* • dítł'o - *it is fuzzy or hairy* • ii - *the one*

Literally fuzzy mountain. This promontory, so named because of its sparse and stunted tree growth, is situated about 2 miles east of Red Lake (Be'ek'id Halchíí'), on the western slope of the Chuska (Ch'óshgai) range.

Gallegos Canyon, New Mexico: Teeł Sikaad
teeł - *cattails, reeds* • sikaad - *a bush, tree, or clump of vegetation in position or spread out*

Cattails spread out. The canyon is a conduit for a stream that enters the San Juan River (Tooh, Tooh Biką'í, Nóóda'í Bitooh, Są Bitooh) about 4 miles east of Farmington (Tóta'). The name derives from a small swampy area near the old Gallegos trading post.

Gallinas, New Mexico: Dził Deez'á
dził - *mountain* • deez'á - *it extends, lies (a mesa, ridge, or bluff)*

An extended mountain or mesa ridge. Gallinas (*chickens*, in Spanish) is a small community on the north side of the Jemez Mountains (Dził Łizhinii).

Gallo Canyon, New Mexico: Ńdíshchíí' Haazt'i'
ńdíshchíí' - *pine tree(s)* • haazt'i' - *it extends upward in a thin line*

Pine trees extend upward in a thin line. This canyon enters Chaco Canyon (Tsé Bíyah Anii'áhí) east of Pueblo Bonito (also Tsé Bíyah Anii'áhí) from the north. There were formerly ponderosa pine trees in the canyon.

Gallup, New Mexico: Na'nízhoozhí
na'nízhoozh - *a bridge* • í - *the place*

The place of the bridge. The Navajo name refers to the old Third Street bridge spanning the Rio Puerco on the north side of town. The English name is after David L. Gallup, a paymaster for the A&P Railroad. Gallup, in northwestern New Mexico, is a busy trading center known for its annual summer Inter-Tribal Indian Ceremonial.

Gallup-UNM Branch College: Na'nízhoozhídi Wódahgo Ólta'ígíí
Na'nízhoozhí - *place of the bridge, Gallup* • di - *at* • wódahgo - *upper, higher* • ólta' - *school* • ígíí - *the one*

The upper school at the place of the bridge. This Gallup campus of the University of New Mexico is situated about ½ mile southeast of the Indian Health Service Hospital (Azee'ál'į Hótsaaí) in Gallup.

Gallup Chamber of Commerce: Adláanii Da'ałchoozhígí
adláanii - *drinkers, drunkards* • da'ałchoozh - *they graze* • í - *the ones* • gi - *at*

The place where the drinkers graze. This old Navajo name alludes to a former cool and grassy area beside the Chamber of Commerce where one might sleep off a night on the town.

Gallup - UNM Branch College: Na'nízhoozhidi Wódahgo Ólta'igíí

Gallup Hogback: Ałnaashii Háálíní

ałnaashii - *on opposie sides* • háálį - *to flow up and out* • (n)i - *the place*

The place where it flows up and out on opposite sides. The hogback is situated immediately to the east of Gallup. This striking monocline extends southward from La Mesa de los Lobos (Dził) for some 15 miles to Nutria (Tsé Dijįhí).

Gambler's Spring, New Mexico: Nááhwiiłbįįhí Bitooh

nááhwiiłbįįhí - *the one who won them again and again (The Gambler)* • bi - *his, hers, its* • tooh - *spring, water, river*

The spring of the one who won them again and again. The name refers to The Gambler of Navajo legend who won all, including the people. The spring is in Chaco Canyon (Tsé Bíyah Anii'áhí).

Gambler's Trail, New Mexico: Nááhwiłbįįhí Bitiin

nááhwiiłbįįhí - *The Gambler (see gloss on Gambler's Spring, directly above)* • bi - *his, hers, its* • (a)tiin - *trail, path*

The trail of The Gambler. This trail in Chaco Canyon (Tsé Bíyah Anii'áhí) leads to Gambler's Spring (Nááhwiiłbįįhi Bitooh).

Gamerco, New Mexico: Łigaiyaa'áhi

łigai - *it is white* • yaa'á - *it sticks up, extends upward* • (h)i - *the one*

The white one that points or extends upward. The Navajo name defines the towering white concrete chimney that dominates the site of the old Gallup-American Coal Company just north of Gallup (Na'nízhoozhí) on Highway 666.

Ganado, Arizona: Lók'aahnteel
lók'aa' - *reeds, cattails* • (d)ah - up, elevated • nteel - *wide*
Wide reeds up at an elevation. Ganado was one of the first points of trading activity on the Reservation. A small trading company was established near Ganado Lake (Be'ek'id Hatsoh) in 1871. The community was named after Navajo chief Ganado Mucho (Spanish, *much livestock*). Ganado Mucho's Navajo name was *Tótsohnii Hastiin* (Big Water Man, or Mr. Big Water). The village is 40 miles north of Chambers (Ch'ilzhóó').

Ganado Lake, Arizona: Be'ek'id Hatsoh
be'ek'id - *lake* • ha - *space, area* • tsoh - *it is big, large*
Big Lake. The lake is just northeast of the settlement of Ganado (Lók'aahnteel).

Gap, Arizona: Yaaniilk'id
yaa - *down, downward* • niilk'id - *a hill that runs to a point and stops*
A downward sloping hill that runs to a point and stops. The gap is in a sandstone ridge 40 miles north of Cameron (Na'ní'á Hayázhí) See *Cedar Ridge, Arizona.*

Giant's Chair, Arizona: Kits'iilí
ki (kin) - *house, building* • ts'iil - *shattered, broken, fragmented* •
í - *the one*
A broken or shattered house. Also, potsherds. This volcanic plug rises from the desert some 10 miles southwest of the Hopi village of Shungopavi (Kin Názt'i'). There are 14th century Hopi ruins south of the plug. The name *Kits'iilí* is also given to Keet Seel, a ruin in Navajo National Monument, Arizona.

Gobernador Knob, New Mexico: Ch'óol'í'í
The exact meaning of this name is obscure, It possibly has pertinence to fir trees (ch'ó). The knob protrudes from barren country near Largo Canyon (Tsíid Bii' Tó). This formation is one of the inner sacred mountains of the Navajo. It is also known as *Ntł'iz Dziil* (Hard Goods Mountain).

Gossip Hills, New Mexico: Aseezí
The word *aseezí* means *gossip, rumor, news.* The site is about 15 miles north of Gallup (Na'nízhoozhí) and east of the old Twin Lakes (Báhástł'ah) day school. These small hills were evidently gathering places where local small talk took place.

Gouldings, Arizona: Tségiizh
tsé - *rock* • giizh - *cut or gap*
Rock gap. Harry Goulding opened a trading post here in 1926. Once considered a very remote outpost, the site now has a landing strip and a cafeteria. It is a couple of miles west of the entrance to Monument Valley (Tsé Bii' Ndzisgaii).

Grand Canyon, Arizona: Tsékooh Hatsoh
tsé - *rock* • (bi)kooh - *canyon* • ha - *space, area* • tsoh - *large, big*
A rock canyon of great area or space. This vast, magnificent canyon, cut through by the Colorado River, also carries the Navajo name Bidáá Ha'azt'i' (a slender line running up to its edge), which alludes to a railroad track running along the canyon rim. Yet another name for the canyon is *Tsélché'ékooh* (red rock canyon).

Grand Falls, Arizona: Adahiilíni
adah - *down, downward from a height* • hiilį - *to flow* • (n)i - *the place*

Downward flowing water. The waterfall, 12 miles downstream from Leupp (Tsiizizii), in the Little Colorado River, is dry much of the year.

Grants, New Mexico: **Naatooh Sik'ai'í**
Naatooh - *Isleta Indian* • sik'ai' - *in position with legs spread* • í - *the one*
The spread-legged Isleta. The reference here is to an Isleta prostitute who practiced her trade here during Grants' earlier times. Grants is 60 miles east of Gallup (Na'nízhoozhí) on U.S. I-40 at the southwest base of Mount Taylor (Tsoodził).

Gray Mountain, Arizona: **Dził Łibáí**
dził - *mountain* • łibá - *it is gray* • í - *the one*
The mountain that is gray. Gray mountain is located 8 miles southwest of Cameron (Na'ní'á Hayázhí). See *Coconino Point and Plateau, Arizona.*

Gray Mountain Wash, Arizona: **Dził Łibáí Bikooh**
dził - *mountain* • łibá - *it is gray* • í - *the one* • bikooh - *wash, arroyo, canyon*
The wash of a gray mountain. This wash is situated at the confluence of the Colorado and Little Colorado Rivers about 15 miles northwest of Cameron, (Na'ní'á Hayázhí).

Greasewood, Arizona: **Díwózhii Bii' Tó**
díwózhii - *greasewood (Atriplex canscens)* • bii' - *in it, within it* • tó - *water, spring*
A spring in the greasewood. Greasewood, where there is a day school, is 20 miles southwest of Ganado (Lók'aahnteel), in the valley of the Pueblo Colorado Wash.

Groaning Lake, Arizona: **Be'ek'id Di'ní**
be'ek'id - *lake* • di'ní - *it groans* • (n)í - *the one*
The lake that groans. Evidently this small lake some 8 miles southwest of Chinle (Ch'ínílí) sometimes emits groaning sounds when it contains water, which is seldom.

Guadalupe Canyon, New Mexico: **Tséyi' Hayázhí**
tsé - *rock* • yi' - *in, within* • tséyi' - *a canyon* • ha - *space, area* • yázhí - *small, little*
Small canyon. The canyon runs from the Cebolleta Mountains, which are an adjunct to Mount Taylor (Tsoodził), eastward to join the Rio Puerco of the East about 2 miles south of the village of Guadalupe.

Hano, Arizona: **Naashashí**
naa (anaa') - *enemy, enemies* • shash - *bear* • í - *the one(s)*
Bear enemies. The Navajo name derives from the use of sand paintings depicting a bear. Hano is a Hopi-Tewa village situated on top of First Mesa, in the Hopi (Ayahkinii) complex of villages.

Hard Rock, Arizona: **Tsé Dildǫ'í**
tsé - *rock* • dildǫ' (dildon) - *it pops, explodes, crackles, bursts* • í - *the one*
Popping or exploding rock. The rock, a porous Cretaceous sandstone of the Mesa Verde group, absorbs water and when heated may loudly explode and fly apart. It abounds in Navajo country (Diné Bikéyah) and is assiduously avoided for use in heating the sweatbath (táchééh). Hard Rock is north of Oraibi (Oozéí).

Haystacks, Arizona: Tséta' Ch'ééch'i

tsé - *rock(s)* • ta' - *between* • ch'éé (ch'é, ch'i) - *out, outward* • ch'i - *wind blows* (note that the difference between *ch'i* here and *ch'í* in the previous gloss is tonal, with a difference in meaning, thus phonemic).

Wind blows out from between rocks. These haystack-form sandstone apparitions stand north of Highway 264, just east of Window Rock (Tséghahoodzání).

Hogback, New Mexico: Tsétaak'á

tsé - *rock* • taa - *into water* • k'á (dik'á) - *it slants, is slanted, tilted*

Rock that slants or tilts into water. This strikingly prominent monocline runs northeastward from near Bennett Peak (Tsé Naajiin) to a point 8 miles east of the community of Shiprock (Naat'áanii Nééz). It is so named because of its proximity, in its northern reaches, to the San Juan River (Tooh, Tooh Biką'í, Nóóda'í Bitooh, Są́ Bitooh).

Hogback Gap, Gallup, New Mexico: Tsé Ałch'į' Naak'ání

tsé - *rock* • ałch'į - *toward each other* • naa - *downward* • k'á - *it slants, is slanted, tilted* • (n)í - *the place*

Where rocks slant or tilt down toward each other. This gap in the Gallup hogback formation was and is used as a pass for old Highway 66. It is also called *Tsé Ałch'į' Náá'áhí* (rocks hanging toward each other) and *Ałnaashii Háálíní* (the place where it flows up and out on opposite sides). See *Gallup Hogback, Gallup, New Mexico.*

Holbrook, Arizona: T''iisyaakin

t'iis - *cottonwood tree(s)* • yaa - *beneath, underneath* • kin - *house(s), building(s)*

Houses under cottonwood trees. Holbrook is a prominent tourist center and cattle and lumber shipping location. It is about 18 miles northeast of The Petrified Forest (Sahdiibisí, Tsé Nástánii).

Hopi Villages, Arizona: Ayahkinii

ayah - *underground* • kin - *house(s)* • ii - *the ones*

The underground house ones, underground house people. The reference is to underground kivas. The Hopi villages are in the high mesa country of northern Arizona, some 50 miles north of Winslow (Béésh Sinil). The ancestors of the Hopi may have lived in the area since the 8th century A.D. The western Navajos call the Hopi *Oozéí,* the name for the village of Oraibi.

Hoskaninii Mesa, Arizona: Hashké Neiniihii

hashké - *he is mean, angry, fierce* • neiniih - *he passes it or them out, around, distributes it or them* • ii - *the one*

The one who passes out or metes out anger. Another possible rendition is, *he distributes it or them angrily.* The mesa is named for a Navajo who evaded Kit Carson in the canyon country and, as did many of his tribesmen, amassed sheep which he held to be given away to the Navajos returning from captivity at Fort Sumner (Hwéeldi). Hoskaninii Mesa is near Monument Valley (Tsé Bii' Ndzisgaii).

Hosta Butte, New Mexico: Ak'i Dah Nást'ání

ak'i - *on, upon* • dah - *up at an elevation, height* • nást'á - *it extends (a mountain ridge or mesa rim)*

A mountain ridge extends along on it up at an elevation. This is a broad sandstone butte near Pinedale (Tó Bééhwiisganí) and Mariano Lake (Be'ek'id Hóteelí), about 20 miles northeast of Gallup (Na'nízhoozhí).

Hoteville, Arizona: Tł'ohchintó
tł'oh - *grass* • chin - *smell, it smells* • tł'ohchin - *wild onion (Allium cernuum)* • tó - *water, spring*

Wild onion spring. Hotevilla is a Hopi village situated on Third Mesa, 8 miles northwest of Oraibi (Oozéí).

Houck, Arizona: Mą'ii To'í
mą'ii - *coyote* • to' - *water, spring* • í - *the place*

Coyote watering place, coyote spring. This small community is on U.S. I-40, about 10 miles east of Sanders (Lichíí' Deez'áhí), near the Arizona-New Mexico state line.

Howell Mesa, Arizona: Tsin Bił Dah Azkání
tsin - *tree(s)* • bił - *with, accompanying* • dah - *up, elevated* • azką - *flat topped* • dah azką - *mesa* • (n)í - *the one*

A mesa with trees on top. The mesa is in the Hopi Reservation (Ayahkinii, Oozéí), on the Moenkopi Plateau. It is also called Cedar Mesa. It was named for E.E. Howell, a geologist with the Wheeler survey party.

Hubbell's Trading Post, Arizona: Jééhkał Binaalyéhé Bá Hooghan
jééhkał - *deaf* • bi - *his, her, its* • naalyéhé - *goods* • bá - *for them* • hooghan - *home* • naalyéhé bá hooghan - *trading post*

The deaf one's trading post. This historic trading post in Ganado (Lók'aahnteel), was founded in 1876 by Lorenzo Hubbell, who is buried on a hill near his store. The trading post is presently administered by the National Park Service.

Huerfano, New Mexico: Hanáádlį
ha - *up, out* • náá - *again, another* • (d)lį - *it flows*

It flows up out again. See *Carson's, New Mexico*, another name for the same site.

Huerfanito, New Mexico: Dził Ná'oodiłii Chílí
dził - *mountain* • ná'oodił - *people move or circle around it* • ii - *the one* • chílí - *small*

Small mountain around which people move. This small mesa is similar in appearance to Huerfano Mountain (Dził Ná'oodiłii). It is about 10 miles northeast of Huerfano (Hanáádlį), on the west side of Blanco Canyon (T'iistah Diiteelí).

Huerfano Mountain, New Mexico: Dził Ná'oodiłii
dził - *mountain* • ná'oodił- *people circle or move around it* • ii - *the one*

The mountain around which people move. In Navajo mythology people circled around this mesa, a steep-walled prominence dominating the country some 30 miles southeast of Farmington (Tóta'). This is one of the sacred mountains of the Navajo, who also call it ceremonially *Yódí Dziil* (Valuable Goods Mountain).

Hunter's Point, Arizona: Tsé Náshchii'
tsé - *rock* • ná - *describing a circle* • (sh)chii' - *red*

Red rock circle. This site is about 7 miles south of St. Michaels (Ts'íhootso), Arizona. The west side of the point contains alternate layers of red and buff sandstone, and the mesa forms a broad curve.

Hubbell's Trading Post, Arizona: Jééhkał Binaalyéhé Bá Hooghan

Ignacio, Colorado: Bíina

The meaning of this Navajo name is uncertain. It is possibly derived from Spanish *pino*, pine. The small community of Ignacio is situated about 20 miles east of Durango (Kin Łání). It is an agricultural area and also the location for a Ute Indian boarding school.

Indian Wells, Arizona: Tó Hahadleeh

tó - *water* • hahadleeh - *pulled out one after the other*

Buckets or pots of water are pulled out one after another. The well was dug by Navajos for camping and other watering purposes. The site is 40 miles north of Holbrook (T'iisyaakin) under the rim of a volcanic tableland.

Inscription House, Arizona: Ts'ah Bii' Kin

ts'ah - *sagebrush (Artemesia tridentata)* • bii' - *in, within* • kin - *house*

House in the sagebrush. Inscription House is a pueblo ruin near Shonto (Sháá'tóhí), 40 miles north of Tuba City (Tó Naneesdizí). The ruins, containing 48 rooms, are part of Navajo National Monument.

Intermountain School, Utah: Dził Biyi' Ólta'

dził - *mountain(s)* • biyi' - *in, within* • ólta' - *school*

School within mountains. Intermountain School is at Brigham City. The school is also rendered as *Dziłyi' Ólta'*, same meaning.

28

Isleta Pueblo, New Mexico: Naatoohí
naa (naa') - *enemy* • tooh - *river* • i - *the place*
The place where the enemies are near the river. The Navajos were traditional enemies of the Isleta and figured prominently in Isleta witchcraft. Isleta is a village situated on both banks of the Rio Grande River (Tooh Ba'áadii, Naakaii Bitooh) 15 miles south of Albuquerque (Bee'eldíildahsinil), not far from its site in 1540 when discovered by the Spaniards.

Iyanbito, New Mexico: Ayání Bito'
ayání - *buffalo, bison* • bi - *his, her, its* • to' - *water, spring*
Buffalo water or spring. The community is about 14 miles east of Gallup (Na'nízhoozhí) and north of U.S. I-40. The name refers to the presence of buffalo imported for an early Gallup Ceremonial. A previous name for the site was *Tł'ízí Łigai* (White Goats).

Jacob's Well, Arizona: Ahoyoolts'ił
a - *away* • ho - *thing, something, it* • yoolts'ił - *it crumbles, cracks*
Something crumbles away. The reference here is probably to a well or hole that grows in size as its walls shatter or crumble away. Van Valkenburg reported in 1940 that 20 years previously Navajos told that the well was "3 saddle ropes or 90 feet across and some 90 feet deep. Today (ca. 1940) the depth is 10 feet and the circumference is ¼ mile." The site is 15 miles south of Sanders (Lichíí' Deez'áhí).

Jemez Mountains, New Mexico: Dził Łizhinii
dził - *mountain(s)* • łizhin - *black* • ii - *the one(s)*
Black mountain or mountains. The Jemez Mountains rise just to the west of the Rio Grande River (Tooh Ba'áadii, Naakaii Bitooh), about 30 miles west of Santa Fe. In the center of this range is a massive extinct volcanic crater, some 10 miles across. Mount Taylor (Tsoodził), another extinct volcano, lies 60 miles to the southwest.

Jemez Pueblo, New Mexico: Mą'ii Deeshgiizh
mą'ii - *coyote* • deeshgiizh - *gapped, having a gap or pass*
Coyote pass. The pueblo is on the east bank of the San Jose River, approximately 35 miles northwest of Albuquerque (Bee'eldíildahsinil). The pass for which the pueblo is named is about 8 miles to the north of the pueblo.

Jet Mountain, Colorado: Bááshzhinii Dziil
bááshzhinii - *jet* • dziil - *mountain*
Jet mountain or mountain made of jet. This is a ceremonial name for the La Plata Mountains (Dibé Ntsaa) in Colorado. The mountains rise north of Durango (Kin Łání).

Jones Ranch, New Mexico: Jééhkał
jééh - *ear, into the ear* • kał - *closed*
Closed ears, deaf. This is a sobriquet applied to a settler or trader in the area. The site is some 25 miles southwest of Gallup (Na'nízhoozhí).

Joseph City, Arizona: Náyaaseesí
ná (anáá') - *eye* • yaa - *beneath, under* • sees - *wart* • i - *the one*
The one with a wart under the eye. The name possibly originates from a partial description of a merchant or trader in the town. This Mormon town is 11 miles west of Holbrook (T'iisyaakin).

Kaibito, Arizona: K'ai' Bii' Tó

k'ai' - *willow(s)* • bii' - *in, within it, them* • tó - *water*

Spring in the willows. Kaibito is in the southern branch of Navajo Canyon (Tsékooh Niitsi̜'ii), about 40 miles northeast of Tuba City (Tó Naneesdizí).

Kayenta, Arizona: Tó Dínéeshzhee'

tó - *water* • dínéeshzhee' - *it fans out as fingers or rivulets*

Waters spread out in rivulets, fan-like. Kayenta is the gateway to Monument Valley (Tsé Bii' Ndzisgaii). It is about 25 miles northeast of Shonto (Shą́ą́'tóhí).

Keams Canyon, Arizona: Lók'a'deeshjin

lók'a' - *reeds* • deeshjin - *a rim or ridge of black extends*

A black ridge of reeds extends. Established in 1880 as a ranch and trading post by Englishman Thomas Keam, this deep canyon community is 60 miles north of Holbrook (T'iisyaakin).

Keet Seel, Arizona: Kits'iilí

ki (kin) - *house(s)* • ts'iil - *fragment, sherd* • í - *the place*

The place of the shattered houses. Keet Seel is the site of an Anasazi ruin in Navajo National Monument.

Kin Bineola, New Mexico: Kin Bii' Naayolí

kin - *house, building* • bii' - *in it* • naayolí - *the wind blows about*

A house in which the wind blows about. This Anasazi ruin is in the Chaco Canyon (Tsé Bíyah Anii'áhí) complex.

Kinbito (Kinnebito), New Mexico: Giní Bit'ohí

giní - *hawk* • bi - *its* • t'oh - *nest* • í - *the one*

Hawk's nest. The settlement is on the north bank of the Kinbito Wash, about 10 miles northeast of Chaco Canyon (Tsé Bíyah Anii'áhí).

Kin Kletso, New Mexico: Kin Łitsooí

kin - *house(s)* • łitso(o) - *yellow* • í - *the one(s)*

Yellow house or houses. This is the site of an Anasazi ruin in Chaco Canyon (Tsé Bíyah Anii'áhí).

Kin Klizhin, New Mexico: Kin Łizhiní

kin - *house(s)* • łizhin - *black* • í - *the one(s)*

Black house or houses. The stone used in the ruin was small, dark brown sandstone, hence the name *Kin Łizhin*. The site is in a side canyon of Chaco Canyon (Tsé Bíyah Anii'áhí).

Kinlichee, Arizona: Kin Dah Łichí'í

kin - *house(s)* • dah - *up, up at an elevation* • łichí'í - *red, it is red*

Red house up at an elevation. The site is 12 miles east of Ganado (Lók'aahnteel). A small Anasazi ruin is located here.

Kit Carson's Cave, New Mexico: Tsé'áhálzhiní

tsé - *rock* • tsé'á (tsé'áán) - *rock cave* • hálzhin - *it is black* • í - *the place*

The place of the blackened-rock cave. The cave has been blackened by the many fires built within it. It is said to have sheltered Kit Carson during his Navajo campaign in the 1860s. This steep, shallow cavern is about 15 miles northeast of Gallup (Na'nízhoozhí).

Kin Bineola, New Mexico: Kin Bii' Naayolí

Klagetoh, Arizona: Łeeyi'tó
lee (łeezh) - *ground, soil, earth* • yi' - *in, within* • tó - *water, spring*

Water or spring in the ground. Klagetoh is situated in a small west-sloping basin 23 miles north of Chambers (Ch'ilzhóó'). There is a trading post and a day school in the community.

Laguna, New Mexico: Tó Łání
tó - *water, spring* • łání - *much, many*

Much water. The pueblo once had a nearby large lake which is now meadowland. Laguna is Spanish for *lake*. This community is 46 miles west of Albuquerque (Bee'eldíildahsinil), near U.S. I-40. It was established in 1697 by Keres Indians fleeing the Spaniards after the Pueblo Rebellion of 1680.

Lake Powell, Arizona, Utah: Tólá Dah Siyíní
tó - *water* • łá - *much* • dah - *up, elevated* • siyį - *a large body of water lies* • (n)í - *place*

Where a large body of water lies at an elevation. The term depicts the water dammed at Page (Na'ní'á Hótsaa) to form the vast lake. Another name, *Kéyah Nihoneel'ání* (where the land extends down to the edge), suggests the land at the edge of the lake to be the northern terminus of the Navajo reservation.

31

Lake Powell, Arizona, Utah: Tólá Dah Siyín

Lake Valley, New Mexico: Be'ek'id Halgaii
be'ek'id - *lake* • ha - *space, area* • (l)gai - *white, it is white* • i - *the place*

White lake. This shallow mesa and grassland site is about 25 miles north of Crownpoint and aproximately 5 miles west of Chaco Canyon (Tsé Bíyah Anii'áhí).

La Plata Mountains, Colorado: Dibé Ntsaa
dibé - *sheep* • ntsaa - *big, large*

Big sheep. This Navajo sacred mountain of the north is so named either because of the Rocky Mountain sheep roaming its ranges or because of its snow-covered resemblance, from a great distance, to a flock of large sheep. Both versions are current. The mountain is also known as *Dził Bíni' Hólóonii* (The Mountain with a Mind), and *Bááshzhinii Dziil* (Jet Mountain). The La Plata Mountains range 50 miles north and south , from Silverton, Colorado to Mesa Verde (Gad Deelzhah, Nóóda'i Dził).

Largo Canyon, New Mexico: Tsíid Bii' Tó
tsíid - *coal, ember* • bii' - *in it, in them* • tó - *water, spring*

Water in the embers. This is the name for the lower section of the canyon. The Navajos call the upper section *Ahidazdiigai* (treeless areas converge or come together). The Franciscan Fathers named the whole canyon *Taahóóteel* (a wide strip of land extending down into the water). The canyon heading is near Regina, New Mexico and enters the San Juan River (Tooh, Tooh Bika'í, Nóóda'i Bitooh, Sá Bitooh) at Blanco (Taahóóteel), New Mexico.

32

Leupp, Arizona: Tsiizizii
tsiiziz - *scalp(s), scalplock(s)* • ii - *the place*

The place of scalps. In one version of this name the Navajos are reputed to have taken Yavapai scalps here. The other story relates that a government agent who worked here wore a wig. The site is about 30 miles northwest of Winslow (Béésh Sinil). The English name is for Francis Leupp, Commisioner for Indian Affairs, 1905 -1908.

Leyit Kin, New Mexico: Łeyi' Kin
łee (łeezh) - *soil, ground* • yi' - *in, within* • kin - *house, building*

House in the ground. This is an Anasazi ruin in Chaco Canyon. (Tsé Bíyah Anii'áhí).

Little Colorado River, Arizona: Tółchi'íkooh
tó - *water* • łchi'í (łichi'í) - *red, it is red* • (bi)kooh - *wash, arroyo*

Red water wash. An important irrigation source for Navajo farming, the river floods in the spring and runs red due to the salmon-colored soil. It dries up in the summer. The Little Colorado heads in Apache County and courses northwestward until it joins the Colorado River in the Grand Canyon (Tsékooh Hatsoh, Bidáá' Ha'azt'i') north of San Francisco Peak (Dook'o'oosłííd).

Little Asaayi Lake, New Mexico: Asaa'yázhí
asaa' - *bowl, pot, kettle* • yázhí - *small, little*

Small bowl. This lake is east of Asaayi Lake (Asaayi') on the western slopes of the Chuska Mountains (Ch'óshgai).

Little White House Canyon, Arizona: Tséyi' Hats'ózí
tséyi' - *canyon* • ha - *space, area* • ts'ózi - *narrow, slender*

Narrow canyon. The canyon, south of Chinle (Ch'ínílį), contains a small 12th century Anasazi ruin roughly resembling White House Ruin (Kinii' Na'ígai) in Canyon de Chelly (Tséyi').

Lizard Spring, Arizona: Na'ashǫ'iito'í
na'shǫ'ii - *lizard, serpent, reptile* • to' - *water, spring* • í - *the place*

Lizard water place, lizard spring. The site is about 10 miles west of Ganado (Lók'aahnteel).

Lokasakad, Arizona: Lók'aa' Sikaad
lók'aa' - *reed(s)* • sikaad - *in position or spread out*

Reeds in position or spread out. This spring is about 25 miles south of Keam's Canyon (Lók'a'deeshjin) and 3 miles west of Bidahochi (Bidahóóchii').

Long Lake, New Mexico: Be'ek'id Hóneezí
be'ek'id - *lake* • hó - *space, area* • neez - *long, tall* • í - *the one*

Literally long lake. This sizeable lake is in the Chuska Range (Ch'óshgai), north of Whiskey Lake (Tódiłhił) and about 4 miles south of Washington Pass (Béésh Łichíi'ii Bigiizh).

Los Gigantes, Arizona: Tsé Ch'ídeelzhah
tsé - *rock(s)* • ch'í - *out, outward* • deelzhah - *jagged, craggy*

Jagged or craggy rocks extending out. These large stone presences lie in desert country south of Hopi (Ayahkinii, Oozéí) Second Mesa near Dilcon (Tsézhin Dilkǫǫh).

Lukachukai, Arizona: Lók'a'ch'égai
lók'aa' - *reeds* • ch'é (ch'i) - *extending out* • gai - *white*
Reeds extending out white. Lukachukai is situated at the west base of the Lukachukai Mountains, about 10 miles north of Tsaile (Tséhílí). The first trading post was established here in 1892. This is also the name of a sheep breeding laboratory located a couple of miles west of Fort Wingate (Shash Bitoo'), New Mexico.

Lupton, Arizona: Tsé Dijoolí
tsé - *rock* • dijool - *round, spherical* • í - *the place*
Round rock. This small settlement is 28 miles west of Gallup (Na'nízhoozhí) in the valley of the Rio Puerco of the West near dramatic red sandstone rocks and cliffs. The site is also known as *Tsé Si'ání* (sitting rock).

Lybrooks, New Mexico: Tó Náálíní
tó - *water* • náá - *down, downward* • lį - *it flows* • (n)í - *the place*
The place where water flows downward. This site, the Lybroooks Ranch, is 10 miles northwest of Counselors (Bilagáana Nééz) on New Mexico Highway 44 at the southern end of the Cibola Mesa. Tree ring data date some of the old Navajo campsites from 1720-1760.

The Mall, Gallup, New Mexico: Bii' Haazhdiilwo'ii
bii' - *in, within* • haa(zh) - *up, around (a path or corridor)* • diilwo' - *to move rapidly, briskly, to run* • ii - *the place*
The place inside where brisk walking or running around is done. The mall is on the northwest side of Gallup (Na'nízhoozhí).

Mancos Creek, Colorado: Tó Nts'ósíkooh
tó - *water* • nts'ósí - *slim, slender, narrow* • (bi)kooh - *canyon, arroyo*
Slim water canyon, narrow canyon. This stream flows from the La Plata Mountains (Dibé Ntsaa) and enters the San Juan River (Tooh, Tooh Bika̧'í, Nóóda'í Bitooh, Sá Bitooh) 20 miles downstream from the community of Shiprock (Naat'áanii Nééz, Tooh). There are important Anasazi ruins in the canyon, most significantly in Mesa Verde (Gad Deelzhah, Nóóda'í Dził).

Manuelito Canyon, Arizona: Kinyaa Tó Deezlíní
kin - *house* • yaa - *under, beneath* • tó - *water, spring* • deezlį - *to flow along, to start to flow* • (n)í - *the place*
Where a spring flows along beneath the house. The spring runs from the northwest in Arizona to Manuelito (Kin Hóchxó̧'í), New Mexico. The stream evidently ran beneath the hogan of a local Navajo, hence the Navajo name. Manuelito, a renowned Navajo Chief, was known by the Navajo names *Daháanan Baadaani* (Son-in-Law of the Late Texan) and *Ashkii Diyiní* (Holy Boy).

Manuelito, New Mexico: Kin Hóchxó̧'í
kin - *house* • hóchxó̧' - *ugly* • í - *the one*
The name is for an Anasazi ruin near the site. Manuelito is 18 miles west of Gallup (Na'nízhoozhí) on the Rio Puerco of the West. There are many ruins in this area.

Manuelito Spring, New Mexico: Ch'il Haajiní
ch'il - *weed, shrub bush, plant* • haa - *extending outward* • jin - *black* • í - *the one*

Black weeds or bushes extend out. The site is 14 miles east of Tohatchi (Tóhaach'i')
in the desert between Mesa de los Lobos (Dził) and the Chaco Canyon (Tsé Bíyah
Anii'áhí) area. Manuelito reputedly lived at this spring. One of his Navajo names
was, therefore, *Hastiin Ch'il Haajiní* (Mr. Blackweeds). For Manuelito's other Navajo names see *Manuelito Canyon, Arizona.*

Many Coyotes, Arizona: Mą'ii Łání
mą'ii - *coyote(s)* • łání - *many*
Literally many coyotes. The site is some 30 miles southwest of Kayenta (Tó
Dínéeshzhee'), and about 20 miles northwest of the northern rim of Black Mesa
(Dziłíjiin).

Many Farms, Arizona: Dá'ák'eh Halání
dá'ák'eh - *field, farm, cornfield* • halání - *many (over a spacious area)*
Many fields or farms. This agricultural area is about 14 miles north of Chinle
(Ch'ínílí).

Many Ladders, Arizona: Haaz'áí Łání
haaz'áí - *the one that extends up, ladder, staircase* • łání - *many*
Many ladders or steps. The sandstone steps are in Canyon del Muerto (Ane'é Tséyi')
of Canyon de Chelly National Monument (Tséyi').

Mariano Lake, New Mexico: Be'ek'id Hóteelí
be'ek'id - *lake* • hóteel - *it is broad, wide* • í - *the one*
Wide or broad lake. This shallow lake varies in size, sometimes drying out
altogether. It is about 8 miles east of Pinedale (Tó Bééhwíisganí) and 15 miles
northeast of Fort Wingate (Shash Bitoo').

Marsh Pass, Arizona: Bitát'ah Dzígai
bitát'ah - *a cliff, or ledge* • dzi - *extending away into the distance or into*
space • gai - *white* • dzigai - *a white streak extending into the distance*
A white-streaked ledge or cliff extending into the distance. This pass is in the Black
Mountain (Dziłíjiin) area. It begins in Long House Valley and opens to the northwest of Kayenta (Tó Dínéeshzhee'). Marsh Pass is also called *Tsé Yík'áán* (rock
extending with a narrow ledge).

Matthews Peak, Arizona: Tsé Binááyołí
tsé - *rock* • biná(á) - *around it, encircling it* • yoł - *it blows* • í - *the place*
The place where the wind blows around the rock. This peak is also known as *Chézhin
Náshjiní* (lava with a black band around it). It is one of the highest points in the
Chuska-Lukachukai Mountains (Ch'óshgai-Lók'a'ch'égai).

Mesa de los Lobos, New Mexico: Dził
dził - *mountain*
According to Van Valkenburgh this is the name the northern Navajos have given
to this vast mesa. The mesa lies closely to the northeast of Gallup (Na'nízhoozhí)
and separates the valley of the Rio Puerco of the West from the Tohatchi Wash,
a region containing Coyote Canyon (Mą'ii Tééh Yítłizhí) and Standing Rock (Tsé
Íí'áhí).

Mesa Fajada, New Mexico: Tsé Dilyilí
tsé - *rock* • dilyil - *porous* • í - *the one*

Porous rock or stone. Mesa Fajada, or Fajada Butte, as it is also called, rises 4 miles east of Pueblo Bonito (Tsé Bíyah Anii'áhí). The high butte was apparently used for purposes of astronomy by the Anasazi. Pictographs among stones at the top of the column suggest that computations for reckoning the seasons and making other calculations were done using the positions of the sun. Another Navajo name for this mesa is *Tsé Diyin* (sacred or holy rock).

Mesa Santa Rita, New Mexico: Nahoobá
nahoo - *around about* • bá - *it is gray*

Gray around about. A formation that is marked or streaked with gray. This ridge is just north of Zuni Salt Lake (Áshįįh), some 20 miles south of Atarque (Tsé Łichíí', Tsélichíí' Sikaadí, Adáágii). The *Nahoobáanii* (Horizontal Gray-Streak People) clan of the Navajos is said to have originated here. The south side of the ridge or mesa appears, from Salt Lake, as a horizontal gray streak.

Mesa Verde, Colorado: Gad Deelzhah
gad - *juniper tree(s)* • deelzhah - *jagged, craggy*

Jagged juniper trees. This high, rugged mesa is covered with thick stands of juniper and pinyon trees. Mesa Verde rises 11 miles east of Cortez (Tséyaatóhi). It contains some of the most important Anasazi ruins in the southwest. The mesa is also known as *Nóóda'í Dził* (Ute Mountain).

Mesita, New Mexico: Tsé Ch'échii'
tsé - *rock(s)* • ch'é (ch'í) - *out, outward* • chii' - *red*

Rocks extending out red. Mesita is about 6 miles east of Laguna Pueblo (Tó Łání), near U.S. Highway I-40.

Meteor Crater, Arizona: Adah Hosh Łání
adah - *downward, down from a height* • hosh - *cactus, cacti* • łání - *many*

Many cacti coming down from a height. The Navajo name refers to the abundance of cacti growing down into the bowl of crater. The site is 20 miles west of Winslow (Béésh Sinil). The crater was discovered in 1861.

Mexican Hat, Utah: Naakaii Ch'ah
naakai - *they go about, wander* • í - *the ones* • Naakaii - *Mexican(s)* • ch'ah - *hat*

The hat of the ones who wander about. This sandstone pinnacle suggests a Mexican sombrero. Mexican Hat is about 25 miles northeast of Monument Valley (Tsé Bii' Ndzisgaii), Arizona.

Mexican Springs, New Mexico: Naakaii Bito'
naakai - *they go about, wander* • í - *the ones* • Naakaii - *Mexican(s)* • bi - *his, her, its, their* • to' - *water, spring*

The spring of the ones who wander about. The old name reported by Van Valkenburgh was *Naakaii Chįįhí Bito'* (Spring of the long-nosed Mexican). The settlement is 18 miles north of Gallup (Na'nízhoozhí) and 3 miles west of Highway 666 in the foothills approaching the Chuska Mountains (Ch'óshgai).

Mexican Water, Arizona: Naakaii Tó
Naakaii - *Mexican(s), literally the ones who wander about. See glosses directly above.* • tó - *water, spring*

Mexican water or spring. The location is 21 miles northeast of Dennihotso (Deinihootso) in steep, rocky country. Mexican Water is also called *Naakaii Tó Hadayiiznilí* (Mexicans dug a number of wells).

Mexican Trail, Arizona: Naakaii Adáánání
Naakaii - *Mexican(s), literally the ones who wander about. See glosses directly above.* • adááná - *descending, moving downward* • (n)i - *the place*

The place where the Mexicans descend. This trail in Canyon del Muerto (Ane'é Tséyi') is reported to be the one used by a division of Lieutenant Chacon's troops when they attacked Massacre Cave in 1805, killing 70 Navajo women and children. The trail is also known as *Naakaii Bidáánání* (same meaning) and *Naakaii Habitiin* (Mexican trail).

Middle Ridge, New Mexico: Ata' Yilk'idí
ata' - *between* • yilk'id - *a hill extends along, a ridge* • i - *the place*

Between the ridges. The site is about 5 miles north of Gallup (Na'nízhoozhí), between China Springs (K'aa' Łání) and Ya-ta-hey (T'áá Biích'įįdii).

Middle Trail Canyon, Arizona: Ata' Ha'atiin
ata' - *between* • ha - *up out, upward* • 'atiin - *road, trail path*

A trail up out between. This trail is east of Chinle (Ch'ínílį) in Canyon de Chelly (Tséyi').

Mishongnovi, Arizona: Tsétsohk'id
tsé - *rock* • tsoh - *big* • k'id - *hill*

Big rock hill or big boulder hill. This Navajo name also refers to the Hopi villages Shipaulovi and Toreva. The name alludes to the massive boulder at the top of the hill approaching the village of Toreva. Mishongnovi is situated on the eastern ridge of the Second Mesa. The Hopi villages (Ayahkinii, Oozéí) begin 11 miles west of Keams Canyon (Lók'a'deeshjin).

Mocking Bird Canyon, New Mexico: Tsin Łeeh Yi'áhí
tsin - *wood, tree, pole, post* • łeeh - *into the earth or ground* • yi'á - *it sticks, extends* • (h)i - *the place*

Where the post sticks into the earth. The site is also called *Burnt Post Ruin*. Mocking Bird Canyon is west of Gallo Canyon (Ńdíshchíí' Haazt'i') in Chaco Canyon (Tsé Bíyah Anii'áhí).

Moenave, Arizona: Kin Łigaaí
kin - *house, building* • łigaaí - *the one that is white*

White house. Moenavi is 4 miles west of Tuba City (Tó Naneesdizí). Father Graces is reputed to have stayed here at the springs in 1776 when he visited the Havasupai tribe (Góóhníinii).

Moencopi, Arizona: Oozéí Hayázhí
Oozéí - *Oraibi, a Hopi village* • ha - *area, space* • yázhí - *small, little*

Little Oraibi. The Hopi name means *place of running water*. Moencopi is 2 miles southeast of Tuba City (Tó Naneesdizí) on the north side of the Moencoopi wash. The site was formerly occupied by a 15th century Anasazi pueblo. Juan de Onate visited this location in the early 17th century. It is also referred to in Navajo as *Naak'a' K'éédílyéhé* (a place where cotton is planted and raised), which is the Navajo name of the Moencopi wash as well.

37

Monument Canyon, Arizona: Dzaanééz Ch'ibitiin

dzaa (jaa') - *ear(s)* • nééz - *long, tall* • dzaanééz - *mule(s), donkey(s)* • ch'i - *out, outward* • bi - *his, hers, its, their* • (a)tiin - *trail, road, path*

Trail or path where the mules come out. Monument Canyon is one of the appendages of Canyon de Chelly (Tséyi'). It is about 4 miles southeast of Chinle (Ch'inili).

Monument Valley, Arizona and Utah: Tsé Bii' Ndzisgaii

tsé - *rock* • bii' - *in within* • ndzisgaii - *stretches of white areas (clearings).*

Stretches of white areas or clearings within or among the rocks. This vast valley of magnificent red sandstone formations is about 20 miles north of Kayenta (Tó Dinéeshzhee'). It is bisected by the Arizona-Utah state line.

Monument Valley, Arizona and Utah: Tsé Bii' Ndzisgaii

Moqui Buttes, Arizona: Dibé Dah Sitíni

dibé - *sheep* • dah - *up, elevated* • sitį́ - *lying down, reclining*

Sheep lying down on high ground. These formations are volcanic plugs spread over an elevated, grassy plateau about 25 miles northeast of Winslow (Béésh Sinil). They are also called Hopi Buttes.

Mount Taylor, New Mexico: Tsoodził

tsoo (atsoo') - *tongue* • dził - *mountain*

Tongue mountain. This derivation is conjectural, but a possibility. The formation of the timber line of this 11,000 foot peak resembles, on the west side of the mountain, the shape of a tongue. Mount Taylor is the Navajo sacred mountain of the south. It is known ceremonially as *Niłtsá Dziil* (Rain Mountain) and *Dootl'izhii Dziil* (Turquoise Mountain).

Narrow Water, New Mexico: Tó Áłts'óózi

tó - *water* • áłts'óózi - *it is slim, slender, narrow*

Slim or narrow water. This slender stream runs down the west side of the Chuska (Ch'óshgai) range and debouches into Red Lake (Be'ek'id Halchíí').

Nashchitti, New Mexico: Nahashch'idí

nahashch'id - *to dig around, scratch around* • i - *the one*

The one who digs or scratches around, a badger. The name is derived from *Nahashch'idí Bito'* (badger springs), near the site. Nashchitti is about 42 miles north of Gallup (Na'nízhoozhí) on Highway 666. One of the earliest trading posts was established here in 1886.

Natural Bridge, Arizona: Tsé Naní'áhi

tsé - *rock* • naní'á - *reaching across, spanning* • (h)i - *the one*

Rock reaching across. This low sandstone span or bridge is about 4 miles southwest of Fort Defiance (Tséhootsooi). There are Anasazi ruins in the area.

Navajo, New Mexico: Ni'iijíhí

ni'iijííh - *crosscutting by saw is done* • i - *the place*

The place where crosscut sawing is done. This large sawmill, 23 miles north of Window Rock (Tséghahoodzání), is one of the major industries in Navajo country (Diné Bikéyah). It gets much of its raw lumber from the Chuska Mountains (Ch'óshgai). Red Lake (Be'ek'id Halchíí') lies immediately to the west of the sawmill.

Navajo Bridge, Arizona: Na'ní'á Hatsoh

na'ní'á - *something rigid extends across* • ha - *area, space* • tsoh - *large, big*

A large, rigid span. This bridge is also known as Lee's Ferry or Marble Canyon Bridge. It spans the Colorado River on U.S. Highway 89, about 40 miles west of Kaibito (K'ai' Bii' Tó).

Navajo Canyon, Arizona: Tsékooh Niitsį'ii

tsé - *rock* • (bi)kooh - *canyon, arroyo* • tsékooh - *rock canyon* • (a)niitsį' - *cheek* • ii - *the one*

Cheek canyon. The provenience of this curious name is unknown. The great canyon lies 15 miles south and southwest of Navajo Mountain (Naatsis'áán). The lower and main crossing point of the canyon, between Kaibito (K'ai' Bii' Tó) and Navajo Mountain (Naatsis'áán) is called *Ch'áyahí* (armpit). The middle place of crossing is named *Altįį Jik'aashí* (bow smoother), after a shrub. This crossing is southeast of the juncture of the Colorado and San Juan Rivers. The name of the upper crossing of Navajo Canyon, southwest of the juncture of the two rivers, is named *Gishí Bikéyah* (the land of the man called Cane or Stick, Mr. Cane's or Mr. Stick's land).

Navajo Churchrock, New Mexico: Tsé Íí'áhí

tsé - *rock* • íí'á - *it stands, projects upward* • (h)i - *the one*

Standing rock. See *Churchrock Spires, New Mexico.*

Navajo Community College, Arizona: Diné Bi'ólta Wódahgoigíí

diné - *Navajo, man, person* • bi - *his, hers, its* • ólta' - *school* • wódahgo - *up, high, up above* • igíí - *the one*

The Navajos' higher school. This community college is 55 miles north of Window Rock (Tségháhoodzání) and 20 miles east of Chinle (Ch'inilį) at Tsaile (Tsééhílį), in the foothills of the Lukachukai Mountains (Lók'a'ch'égai). The campus is only a few miles from the northern branch of Canyon de Chelly (Tséyi').

Navajo Mountain, Utah: Naatsis'áán
naa (anaa') - *enemy* • tsis (sis) - *mountain* • 'áán (a'áán) - *cave*

Enemy mountain cave. Navajo Mountain, at 10,388 feet, dominates the landscape in this far northwestern part of Navajo country (Diné Bikéyah). It is 25 miles northwest of Kayenta (Tó Dinéeshzhee'), as the crow flies, and just north of the Arizona-Utah border. The mountain was reputedly used as a heliographic signalling point by the U.S. Army during the Navajo wars of 1863-4. The mountain is considered sacred by the Navajos.

Navajo Peak, Colorado: Dził Binii' Ligaii
dził - *mountain* • bi - *his, her, its* • (a)nii' - *face* • ligai - *white* • i - *the one*

The mountain with a white face, white-faced mountain. Navajo Peak, near Chromo, Colorado, is in the San Juan Mountains (Dził Ligaii). It is held sacred by the Navajos.

Navajo Springs, Arizona: Kin Ligaai
kin - *house(s), building(s)* • ligai - *it is white* • i - *the one*

White house or houses. The site is 40 miles east of Holbrook (T'iis Yaakin) on the north side the Rio Puerco of the West. This area was the focal point of many Navajo-White conflicts in the 1880's engendered by U.S. land grants to the Atlantic and Pacific Railroad, now the Santa Fe.

Nazlini, Arizona: Názlíní
názlį - *to flow in a circle, to turn flowing* • (n)i - *the place*

Where the water makes a turn as it flows. Nazlini is 15 miles south of Chinle (Ch'inilį). The area abounds in Anasazi ruins, especially in Nazlini Canyon, up-creek from the community of Nazlini.

Newcomb, New Mexico: Bis Deez'áhí
bis - *clay, adobe* • deez'á - *it extends* • (h)i - *the place*

Where adobe extends. The Newcombs founded a trading post here, 50 miles north of Gallup (Na'nízhoozhí), in 1914.

No Water Mesa, Arizona: Tó Ádin Dah Azką́
tó - *water* • ádin - *to be non-existent* • dah - *up, elevated* • azką́ - *flat topped* • dah azką́ - *mesa, tableland*

A mesa where there is no water. This tableland is a short distance north of Sweetwater (Tó Likani), in northern Arizona.

Nutria, New Mexico: Tsé Dijįhí
tsé - *rock* • dijįh (dijį́h) - *to blacken, turn black* • i - *the one*

Rock that turns black. Nutria (Spanish for *otter*) is a Zuni village about 20 miles northeast of Zuni Pueblo (Naasht'ézhi). Many Navajos live immediately north of Nutria. There was warfare between the Navajos and the Zunis in the late 19th century. The Village of the Great Kivas, an Anaasazi ruin occupied between 1000-30 A.D., is in the Nutria Valley.

40

Oak Ridge, Arizona: **Tséch'il Yilk'id**
tsé - *rock* • ch'il - *plant* • tséch'il - *rock plant, oak* • yilk'id - *a hill extending out, a ridge*
A hill extending out covered with oak. This site is 10 miles north of Pine Springs (T'iis Íí'áhí) and 15 miles south of Ganado (Lók'aahnteel).

Oak Springs, Arizona: **Teeł Ch'ínít'i'**
teeł - *cattails, reeds* • ch'í - *out, outward* • nít'i' - *to extend or stretch horizontally*
Cattails or reeds extending out horizontally. Oak Springs is 7 miles south of Hunter's Point (Tsé Náshchii') and east of the Defiance Plateau. There is a large Anasazi ruin nearby.

Oak Springs Canyon, Arizona: **Tsétł'áán Ńdíshchí'í**
tsé - *rock* • tł'áán - *possibly from* tł'ah, *curved, corner, angular* • ńdíshchíí' - *pinetree(s)* • í - *the place*
Where pine trees are on the curve of the rock or canyon edge. This canyon lies about 20 miles southwest of Window Rock (Tségháhoodzání) between the Defiance Plateau on the west and the smaller East Defiance Monocline on the east. State Road 166 runs through the canyon from Lupton (Tsé Dijoolí), on U.S. I-40, northward to St. Michaels (Ts'íhootso).

Ojo Encino, New Mexico: **Chéch'iizh Bii' Tó**
ché (tsé) - *rock* • ch'iizh - *rough* • bii' - *in it, them* • tó - *water, spring*
Water or spring in or among rough rocks. The name may refer to fallen, crumbled rocks around the spring. The site is some 50 miles northeast of Crownpoint (T'iists'óóz Ńdeeshgizh) and 4 miles north of Star Lake (Chéch'il Dah Łichíí'). The Navajos also call Ojo Encino Chéch'il Dah Łichí'í, nearly the same name given to Star Lake.

Old Coal Mine, Arizona: **Łeejin Hasáni**
łee(zh) - *earth, soil, ground* • jin - *black* • łeejin - *coal* • ha - *area, space* • sáni - *old one, old place*
Old coal place. The site is 25 miles southeast of Tuba City (Tó Naneesdizí) and 20 or more miles west of the Hopi Villages (Ayahkinii, Oozéí).

Old Navajo Inn, New Mexico: **Tó Biyah Anii'áhi**
tó - *water, liquor* • biyah - *under it* • anii'á - *it is supported or braced up* • (h)í - *the place*
Where the liquor is supported or braced up. The reference is to beams supporting the projecting roof over the front of the establishment. This building was situated east of Window Rock (Tséghahoodzání), just over the New Mexico border.

Oljetoh, Utah: **Ooljéé'tó**
ooljéé' - *moon* • tó - *water, spring*
Moon water, moon spring. Water runs out of the wash here and flows into the San Juan River (Tooh, Tooh Bíka'í, Nóóda'í Bitooh, Są Bitooh). Oljetoh lies 24 miles north of Kayenta (Tó Dínéeshzhee').

Oraibi, Arizona: **Oozéí**
Oozéí - *eagle trap (reputed Hopi word)*

41

This Hopi village is on the eastern rim of the Third Mesa . The pueblo is said to be the oldest continuously inhabited village in the United States. The western Navajos call the Hopi Villages *Oozéí*. Another widely used name is *Ayahkinii* (underground ones, underground people). The villages begin about 11 miles west of Keam's Canyon (Lók'a'deeshjin).

Page, Arizona: Na'ní'á Hótsaa
na'ní'á - *something rigid extending across, a rigid span* • hó - *space, area* • (n)tsaa - *it is big, large*

A large, rigid span. The reference is to the bridge and dam spanning the Colorado River at Page. Page, 50 miles northwest of Kaibito (K'ai' Bii' Tó), is on the southwestern shore of Lake Powell (Tólá Dah Siyíní).

Paguate, New Mexico: K'ish Ch'inít'i'
k'ish - *alder trees* • ch'í - *out, outward* • nít'i' - *to extend horizontally in a line*

Alders extend out horizontally. This Laguna Indian community is situated on the southeast slope of Mount Taylor (Tsoodzil), about 8 miles north of Laguna Pueblo (Tó Łání).

Painted Desert, Arizona: Halchíítah
ha - *space, area* • (l)chíí (łichíí') - *it is red* • tah - *among, amidst*

Amidst red spaces or areas. This highly colorful landscape lies 28 miles east of Holbrook (T'iisyaakin) and north of U.S. Highway I-40. The Spanish explorers, impressed by the stunning colors of the area, named it *El Desierto Pintado*, The Painted Desert.

Paiute Canyon, Utah: Tsékooh
tsé - *rock* • (bi)kooh - *canyon*

Rock canyon. The head of the canyon is in the Shonto (Sháá'tóhí) Plateau, about 20 miles southeast of Navajo Mountain (Naatsis'áán), and runs to the north to the San Juan River (Tooh, Tooh Bikạ'í, Nóóda'í Bitooh, Sá Bitooh). The upper crossing of the canyon is called *Bá'azhchíní* (the one born for him). The name of the middle crossing is *Nástł'ah* (cove or corner). The Navajos call the lower crossing *T'iis Náát'i'* (cottonwood hanging down).

Paiute Farms, Utah: Báyóodzin Bikéyah
Báyóodzin - a Navajo rendition of *Paiute* • bi - *his, her, its, their* • kéyah - *land, country*

Paiute land or country. The road to this area is from Oljetoh (Ooljéé'tó). The site is 35 miles south of the juncture of the San Juan (Tooh, Tooh Bikạ'í, Nóóda'í Bitooh, Sá Bikooh) and Colorado (Tó Nts'ósíkooh) Rivers in southern Utah.

Paiute Mesa, Arizona, Utah: Deez'á
deez'á - *it lies extended as a long ridge or bluff*

An elongated ridge or mesa. Paiute Mesa lies next to Paiute Canyon (Tsékooh), 20 miles east of Navajo Mountain (Naatsis'áán) and some 22 miles west of Monument Valley (Tsé Bii' Ndzisgaii).

Penasco Blanco, New Mexico: Táalakin
táala - *flat-topped* • kin - *house, building*

Flat-topped house. This is the Navajo name for a ruin in Chaco Canyon (Tsé Bíyah Anii'áhí), 3 miles south of Pueblo Bonito (also Tsé Bíyah Anii'áhí).

Penistaja, New Mexico: Bíniishdáhí
bínii - *against it* • shdá (sédá) - *I sit* • (h)í - *the one*

I sit against it. The Navajo word mimics the sound of the Spanish one, resulting in a curious meaning. This community is about 15 miles west of Cuba (Na'azísí To'í), New Mexico.

Pescado, New Mexico: Táala Hótsaii
táala - *flat-topped* • hó - *area, space* • (n)tsaa - *large* • ii - *the place*

Large, spacious flat-topped area. This Navajo name probably refers to the abundance of flat-topped mesas in the vicinity. Pescado is a small, scattered Zuni farming community on the banks of a fork in the Zuni River, 13 miles east of Zuni Pueblo (Naasht'ézhí). The Spanish name refers to the fish found in the springs in the area.

Petrified Forest, Arizona: Sahdiibisí
sahdii - *upright, alone* • bis - *adobe, clay* • í - *the place*

The place where there are lone pieces of clay or adobe sticking up. The Navajos also call the site *Tsé Nástánii* (rock logs). Petrified Forest National Monument is a vast desert area lying 25 miles east of Holbrook (T'iisyaakin). It comprises some 40 square miles.

Pinedale, New Mexico: Tó Bééhwíisganí
tó - *water, spring* • béé (biná) - *around* • hwiisgan (hasgan) - *the area is dry* • í - *the place*

Where it is dry around the water. This community is 6 miles northwest of Mariano Lake (Be'ek'id Hóteel) amidst high pinyon and juniper-covered mesas. One of the earliest day schools was established here in 1910.

Pine Haven, New Mexico: Chííh Ntł'izii
chííh - *nose* • ntł'iz - *hard* • ii - *the one*

The one with a hard nose. The site is about 15 miles south of Gallup (Na'nízhoozhí), near the western slopes of the Zuni Mountains. The Navajo name refers to a former trader and merchant of the area.

Pine Springs, Arizona: T'iis Íi'áhí
t'iis - *cottonwood tree* • ii'á - *it stands, projects upward* • (h)í - *the place, the one*

Standing cottonwood. Pine Springs is 7 miles north of Houck (Mạ'ii To'í), in high juniper and pinyon country.

Piñon, Arizona: Be'ek'id Baa Ahoodzání
be'ek'id - *lake* • baa - *in, to, toward* • ahhodzą́ - *there is a hole in it, it is perforated* • (n)í - *the one, the place*

A lake with a hole in it. The hole referred to is evidently a drilled well. The site is on Black Mesa (Dzilíjiin) north of Keams Canyon (Lók'a'deeshjin) and 42 miles west of Chinle (Ch'ínílí).

Polacca, Arizona: Ayahkiní
ayah - *underground* • kin - *house, building* • í - *the ones*

The underground house people. Polacca is one of the Hopi Villages (Ayahkinii). The Navajo name for the Hopi villages is a slight variation of the name for Polacca, and the Hopi village of Sichomovi is called *Ayahkin,* only minimally different from the other two names. All three appelations have about the same meaning. Polacca is 11 miles west of Keams Canyon (Lók'a'deeshjin).

Poncho House, Utah: Tséyaakin
tsé - *rock* • yaa - *under, beneath* • kin - *house, building*

House beneath the rock. Poncho House is an Anasazi cliff ruin of the late Mesa Verde type. The underlying strata provide indications of earlier Anazazi occupation. The ruin is situated about 20 miles north of Mexican Water (Naakaii Tó, Naakaii Tó Hadayiiznili), Arizona.

Public Health Hospital, Gallup, New Mexico: Azee' Ál'į Hótsaaí
azee' - *medicine* • ál'į - *it is made* • hó - *area, space* • (n)tsaa - *big, large* • i - *the place*

The big space where medicine is made or administered. This was also the Navajo name for the old St. Mary's Hospital in Gallup, which was demolished in the 1960's. The general name for any hospital in Navajo is *azee' ál'į* (medicine is made). The Public Health Service Hospital, or Indian Health Service Hospital, is situated in the southern hills of Gallup, near The Gallup -UNM Branch College (Na'nízhoozhídí Wódahgo Ólta'ígíí).

Pueblo Alto, New Mexico: Nááhwiiłbįįhí Bikin
Nááhwiiłbįįhí - *the one who won them again and again (the legendary Gambler)* • bi - *his, her* • kin - *house*

The Gambler's house. The site is also called *Nááhwiiłbįįhí Baghan,* with the same meaning, *baghan* being the possessed form of *hooghan* (house or home). This ruin, whose Spanish meaning is *high village,* is in Chaco Canyon (Tsé Bíyah Anii'áhí). See *Gambler's Spring, New Mexico.*

Pueblo Alto Store, New Mexico: Tsédáá'tóhí
tsé - *rock* • dáá' - *rim, edge* • tó - *water, spring* • (h)i - *the place, the one*

The place where there is a spring at the edge of the rock. The store was in the Pueblo Pintado (Kinteel Ch'inílíní) area of Chaco Canyon (Tsé Bíyah Anii'áhí), about 55 miles north of Crownpoint (T'iists'óóz Ńdeeshgizh).

Pueblo Bonito, New Mexico: Tsé Bíyah Anii'áhí
tsé - *rock* • bíyah - *under it* • anii'á - *it is supported or braced up* • (h)i - *the one, the place*

A rock that is supported by something extending under it, a braced rock. Pueblo Bonito is the principal ruin in Chaco Canyon. This large, impressive site is delta-shaped and contains 800 rooms. The name, which is widely used by the Navajos when referring to Chaco Canyon, identifies the masonry built by the Anasazi to prop up a massive threatening rock behind the pueblo. The rock fell in 1941.

Pueblo del Arroyo, New Mexico: Tábąąhkiní
tá (tó) - *water* • bąąh - *shore, edge* • kin - *house, building* • i - *the place, the one*

Water's edge house. This Anasazi ruin is less than a mile west of Pueblo Bonito (Tsé Bíyah Anii'áhí). Nine kivas are in evidence at the site.

Pueblo Pintado, New Mexico: Kinteel Ch'inílíní
kin - *house, building* • (n)teel - *wide* • ch'i - *out, outward* • níłį - *it flows* • (n)í - *the place, the one*

Where there is an outflow at the wide house. This is the easternmost ruin of Chaco Canyon (Tsé Bíyah Anii'áhí). It lies about 3 miles west of the Pueblo Pintado School (Nihoodeeshgiizh Ch'inílíní).

Pueblo Pintado Canyon, New Mexico: Nihodeeshgiizh
niho - *space extending downward* • deeshgiizh - *gap or cut*

A downward extending pass or gap. Pueblo Pintado Canyon is one of the canyons cutting through and draining the northeastern part of Chacra Mesa (Tségai) at Chaco Canyon (Tsé Bíyah Anii'áhí). This Navajo name also refers to Dalton's Pass, New Mexico. A variant spelling of the term is *Nahodeeshgiizh*, with the same meaning.

Pueblo Pintado School, New Mexico: Nihodeeshgiizh Ch'inílíní
niho - *space extending downward* • deeshgiizh - *a pass or gap* • ch'i - *out, outward* • níłį - *it flows* • (n)í - *the place*

Where water flows out at or near a descending pass. This site is in Chaco Canyon (Tsé Bíyah Anii'áhí) about 3 miles east of the easternmost ruins in the canyon.

Puertocito, New Mexico: T'iistsoh
t'iis - *cottonwood tree(s)* • tsoh - *big*

Big cottonwoods. See *Alamo, New Mexico*.

Pyramid Rock, New Mexico: Tséchį́įhí
tsé - *rock* • chį́įh - *nose* • í - *the one*

Nose rock. This massive, roseate, proboscis-shaped formation dominates the spectacular red rock cliffs 10 miles east of Gallup (Na'nízhoozhí) and just north of the settlement of Churchrock (Kinłitsosinil).

Rainbow Natural Bridge, Utah: Tsé'naa Na'ní'áhí
tsé - *rock* • naa - *across* • na'ní'á - *something rigid extends across, a span or bridge* • (h)í - *the place*

Where rock spans rigidly across. This natural sandstone bridge is in the tortuous canyon region of southeast Utah. Now part of Lake Powell (Tółá Dah Siyíní), it is situated some 12 miles northwest of Navajo Mountain (Naatsis'áán). First known to have been visited by whites (John Wetherill and others), it is now frequented by tourists with motorboats and water skis. *Sic transit gloria mundi.*

Ramah, New Mexico: Tł'ohchiní
tł'oh - *grass* • chin - *smell, it smells* • tł'ohchin - *grass that smells, wild onion (Allium cernuum)* • í - *the place*

The place of wild onions. Ramah, a Mormon settlement, is forty-five miles southeast of Gallup (Na'nízhoozhí) in a pleasant valley bordered by hills and red sandstone cliffs harboring a lake. Many Navajos live in the area.

Raton Springs, New Mexico: Tó Dich'íí'
tó - *water, spring* • dich'íí' - *bitter*

Bitter water. The site is about 5 miles west of Star Lake (Chéch'il Dah Lichíí'). It was once a stopping place on the old Albuquerque (Bee'eldíildahsinil) to Farmington (Tóta') wagon road.

Pyramid Rock, New Mexico: Tséchííh

Rattlesnake, New Mexico: Siláo Habitiin

siláo - *soldier* • ha - *up, upward* • bi - *his, her, their* • (a)tiin - *trail, road*

Soldiers' trail going up. The first word in the Navajo name, a rendition of Spanish *soldado*, is one of the very few words borrowed by Navajo from any language. This site is about 8 miles into the desert south of Shiprock Pinnacle (Tsé Bit'a'í).

Red Lake, New Mexico: Be'ek'id Halchíí'

be'ek'id - *lake* • halchíí' - *the area is red*

Literally a red lake, so named because of the rosy earth colors of the area and the reddish cast they give to the lake waters. Red Lake is 23 miles north of Fort Defiance (Tséhootsooí). It is the site of a large sawmill. The community that has formed around the sawmill is Navajo, New Mexico, which is called *Ni'iijíhí* (sawmill) by the Navajos. The lake is fed by streams from the Chuska Mountains (Ch'óshgai) to the east. Red Lake, Arizona also carries the name *Be'ek'id Halchíí'*.

Red Lake, Arizona: Be'ek'id Halchíí'

be'ek'id - *lake* • halchíí' - *the area is red*

Red lake. This lake is in Coconino County at the northwest corner of the Hopi Reservation (Ayahkinii, Oozéí) near Wildcat Peak (Náshdóits'o'í). Tuba City (Tó Naneesdizí), 22 miles to the southwest, is the nearest community by road.

Red Rock, New Mexico: Tsé Łichíí' Dah Azkání

tsé - *rock* • łichíí' - *it is red* • dah - *up, elevated* • azką́ - *flat-topped* dah azką́ - *mesa* • (n)í - *the place, the one*

The place where there are elevated red, flat-topped rocks. The place of red-rock mesas. The mesas are in rugged territory on the east side of the red sandstone country that links the Lukachukai (Lók'a'ch'égai) and the Carrizo (Dził Náhoozⱡii) Mountains. Red Rock is 15 miles west of Shiprock Pinnacle (Tsé Bit'a'í). The first trading post at Red Rock was built in 1900.

Red Water Standing, New Mexico: Tóⱡichíísiką́

tó - *water* • łichíí' - *it is red* • siką́ - *it stands in an open concavity or depression*

Literally red water standing. This pond in the Chuska Mountains (Ch'óshgai) takes on a red cast toward the afternoon. Surrounded by ponderosa pine, it lies closely southwest of Whiskey Lake (Tódiⱡhiⱡ).

Rehoboth, New Mexico: Tséyaaniichii'

tsé - *rock* • yaa - *downward* • niichii' - *red extends and ends*

Red rock extending downward. The Navajo name defines the stunningly panoramic red sandstone cliffs and other formations 8 miles east of Gallup (Na'nízhoozhí). This great complex of cliffs and bluffs embraces both Pyramid Rock (Tséchį́į́hí) and Churchrock Pinnacles (Tsé Íí'áhí). The community of Rehoboth, to the south of the red rock massif, runs a boarding school, a hospital, and a mission church. The settlement was founded in 1903.

Red Willow Wash, New Mexico: K'ai' Jíchii'

k'ai' - *willows* • jíchii' - *coming out red*

Willows coming out red. This wash descends from the Chuska Peak (Ch'óshgai) area and runs through the village of Tohatchi (Tóhaach'i'), which is 25 miles north of Gallup.

Rio Grande River, Colorado, New Mexico: Tooh Ba'áadii

tooh - *river* • ba (bi) - *his, her, its* • áád - *female* • ii - *the one*

Female river. A variant usage is *Tooh Ba'áád*, with the same meaning. The Rio Grande is also known as *Naakaii Bitooh* (Mexicans' River). The great river rises in the La Plata Mountains (Dibé Ntsaa), east of Silverton, Colorado and flows southward past Albuquerque (Bee'eldííldahsinil), New Mexico into Texas and Mexico.

Rock Point, Arizona: Tsé Łichii' Deez'áhí

tsé - *rock* • łichii' - *it is red* • deez'á - *it is pointed, it extends* • (h)í - *the one*

Pointed or extended red rock. This marvelous area, abounding in red rock formations and canyons, lies 25 miles north of Chinle (Ch'ínílį́) and about 20 miles southwest of the Carrizo Mountains (Dził Náhoozⱡii). The site is named for two prominent sandstone crags. Rock Point is also called *Tsé Ntsaa Deez'áhí* (big pointed or extended rock).

Rock Slide, New Mexico: Tsé Náázhoozhí

tsé - *rock* • náázhoozh - *a mass slid down* • í - *the place*

Where a mass of rock slid down. This avalanche is near Defiance Station (Tsé Ńdeeshgiizh), 6 miles west of Gallup (Na'nízhoozhí).

Rock Springs, New Mexico: Chéch'ízhí

ché (tsé) - *rock* • ch'ízh (ch'íízh) - *rough* • í - *the one*

Rough rock. This location is about 8 miles northwest of Gallup (Na'nízhoozhí). It was on the old army trail of the 1850's from Fort Wingate (Shash Bitoo') to Fort Defiance (Tséhootsooí). Howard Wilson (Náshdóí Yáázh), a cattleman and sheriff, had one of the first ranches in this region. This area was also named *Ts'ah Bii'tóhí* (water or spring in among the sagebrush) when a well was dug in the vicinity. The well additionally bore the name *Wáshindoon Bito'* (Washington water or spring) for the stock dams the Federal Government built there in the early 1930's. Rough Rock, Arizona also carries the Navajo appelation *Chéch'ízhí* or *Tséch'ízhí*.

The Rock Struck By Lightning, Arizona: Tsé Bi'oos'ní'í

tsé - *rock* • bi'oos'ní' - *it was struck by lightning* • í - *the one*

The rock which was struck by lightning. The rock is some 3 or more miles above White House Ruin (Kinii' Na'ígai) in Canyon de Chelly (Tséyi'), on the north side of the canyon. Black streaks run down the sides of this red rock.

The Rock That Water Flows Around, Arizona: Tsé Ná'áz'éli

tsé - *rock* • ná'áz'él (ná'áz'éél) - *something (water) flows around* • í - *the one*

The rock that water flows around. This site is in Monument Canyon (Dzaanééz Ch'íbitiin) in Canyon de Chelly (Tséyi'), about 14 miles southeast of Chinle (Ch'ínílí).

The Rock The Wind Blows Around, New Mexico: Tsé Binááyołí

tsé - *rock* • bináá - *around it* • yoł - *wind blows* • í - *the one*

The rock the wind blows around. This rock spire, a capped sandstone formation in the checkerboard area, lies few miles west of U.S. Highway 666 at the southwest edge of the community of Ya-Ta-Hey (T'áá Bíích'ijdii). The wind comes up the valley from the southwest and swirls around the rock. Matthew's Peak, Arizona also carries the Navajo name *Tsé Binááyołí.*

Rocky Point, Arizona: Tsélchíít'aah

tsé - *rock* • łichíí' - *it is red* • t'aah (t'ah) - *close to, near*

Close to red rock. Rocky point is about 40 miles north of Many Farms (Dá'ákeh Halání), near Rock Point (Tsé Łichíí' Deez'áhí).

Rocky Point, New Mexico: Chézhin Dítł'ooí

ché (tsé) - *rock* • zhin - *black* • chézhin - *lava* • dítł'o - *fuzzy, hairy* • í - *the one*

Fuzzy black rock, fuzzy lava. Named for a volcanic lava plug which sprouts moss and weeds through its many fissures, this formation is about 9 miles west of Gallup (Na'nízhoozhí), on the south side of the Rio Puerco Valley.

Roof Butte, Arizona: Adáá' Dik'á

adáá' - *rim, edge, ledge* • dik'á - *it is slanted*

Slanted rim or edge. This mountain, at 9,575 feet, is the highest point in the Lukachukai Mountains (Lók'a'ch'égai). There is an Indian Forest Service lookout tower and a Navajo Tribal Utility Authority (NTUA) transmission station at the summit. The Navajos also call this site *Dził Dah Neeztínii* (mountain at an elevation reclining). It is a sacred mountain of the tribe.

Rough Rock, Arizona: Tséch'ízhí
tsé - *rock* • ch'ízh (ch'íízh) - *rough* • í - *the one*
Rock that is rough. This is an often-used name in Navajo country (Diné Bikéyah). It is also the name for Rock Springs, New Mexico, among other sites. A variant spelling and pronunciation is *Chéch'ízhí*, with the same meaning. Rough Rock, Arizona, the location of a U.S. Government demonstration school, is about 30 miles northwest of Chinle (Ch'ínílį), at the northeastern base of Black Mesa (Dziłíjiin).

Round Rock, Arizona: Tsé Nikání
tsé - *rock* • niką́ - *concave, bowl-shaped* • (n)í - *the one*
Rock that has a concavity or bowl shape as part of its appearance. The Navajo name probably originates from the impression of concavity in a hole in one of the rocks nearby. The community of Round Rock is 30 miles northeast of Chinle (Ch'ínílį) and some 13 miles west of Cove (K'aabizhii, K'aabizhistł'ah).

Round Rock Trading Post, Arizona: Bis Dootł'izh Deez'áhí
bis - *adobe, clay* • dootł'izh - *it is blue* • deez'á - *it extends as a ridge or bluff* • (h)í - *the place*
Where blue clay extends as a ridge or bluff. The trading post, in the settlement of Round Rock, is 30 miles north of Chinle (Ch'ínílį) and 13 miles west of Cove (K'aabizhii, K'aabizhiistł'ah). In 1892 Superintendent Dana Shipley, who had been zealously rounding up Navajo children for school, was driven by Navajos led by Black Horse to seek refuge in the trading post. He was rescued by cavalry from Fort Defiance (Tséhootsooí).

Sagebrush Liquors (northwest of Gallup), New Mexico: Ts'ah Bii' Njik'ai'í
ts'ah - *sagebrush (Artemesia tridentata)* • bii' - *in it* • njik'ai' - *to walk fork-legged, to stagger about* • í - *the place*
Where one walks fork-legged or staggers about in the sagebrush. This establishment is on the Window Rock (Tséghahoodzání) road west of Ya-Ta-Hey (T'áá Bíích'į́įdii), about 15 miles northwest of Gallup (Na'nízhoozhí).

Salahkai, Arizona: Tséłigai
tsé - *rock* • łigai - *it is white*
White rock or rocks. Salahkai, a mesa in Apache County, lies some 70 miles north of Holbrook (T'iisyaakin) near Salina (Tséláni).

Salina, Arizona: Tséláni
tsé - *rock* • láni (łáni) - *many*
Many rocks. This small community is situated on the east side of Balukai Mesa (Baalók'aa'í), about 25 miles southwest of Chinle (Ch'ínílį).

Salt Point, New Mexico: Áshįįh Náá'á
áshįįh - *salt* • náá'á - *it extends downward*
Salt extends downward. Salt Point is at the juncture of the Largo (Taahóóteel) and Blanco (T'iistah Diteelí) Canyons. There are ruins below this point. Navajos collected salt in earlier times from the sandstone strata at the site.

San Anton Spring, New Mexico: Tó Łitso
tó - *water, spring* • łitso - *it is yellow*

Yellow water. The site is 6 miles northeast of Thoreau (Dłǫ'áyázhí) at the foot of San Anton Hill. There was early Mexican cattle and sheep ranching in this area, which was occupied by 1858.

San Felipe Pueblo, New Mexico: Séí Bee Hooghan

séí - *sand* • bee - *by means of it, with it* • hooghan - *home(s), house(s)*

Houses made of sand. This Keresan-speaking pueblo is 28 miles north of Albuquerque on the east side of the Rio Grande River (Tooh Ba'áadii, Naakaii Bitooh). The pueblo, reputedly the place of origin of the Navajo Black Sheep Clan (Dibé Łizhiní), is also called *Dibé Lizhiní*, as well as *Tsédáá' Kin* (edge of rock houses).

San Fidel, New Mexico: Dził Łeeshch'ihí

dził - *mountain* • łeeshch'ih - *ash, ashes* • (h)í - *the one*

Ash mountain. This mountain is 15 miles southeast of Grants (Naatooh Sik'ai'í) in lava country near U.S. I-40.

San Francisco Peak, Arizona: Dook'o'oosłííd

doo - *not* • k'o (k'i) - *on, upon* • (oos)łííd - *it melts off, runs off*

It has not melted off on top. The reference is to the nearly perennial snows that cover the summit of this mighty peak near Flagstaff (Kin Łání). This is the Navajo sacred mountain of the west. It is also ceremonially called *Dził Ghá'nítts'íílii* (Faultless Mountain) and *Diichiłídziil* (Abalone Shell Mountain).

San Francisco Peak, Arizona: Dook'o'oosłííd

San Ildefonso, New Mexico: Tséta' Kin

tsé - *rock(s)* • ta' - *between* • kin - *house, building*

House between the rocks. The name refers to the area between Round Mountain and Buckman Mesa. The pueblo lies 20 miles north of Santa Fe (Yootó), on the west bank of the Rio Grande River (Tooh Ba'áadii, Naakaii Tooh). A Spanish mission was founded at the pueblo in 1617.

San Juan Pueblo, New Mexico: Kin Ligaaí
kin - *house, building* • ligaaí - *it is white*

White house or houses. San Juan Pueblo is situated on the banks of the Rio Grande River (Tooh Ba'áadii, Naakaii Bitooh) 30 miles north of Santa Fe (Yootó). The name *Kin Ligaaí* is the modern Navajo name for the pueblo. Its old name was *Kin Lichíí'* (red houses), for which, possibly, the Red House Clan (Kin Lichíí'nii) of the Navajos was named. Don Juan de Onate occupied the pueblo in 1598.

The San Juan Mountains, Colorado: Dził Ligaii
dził - *mountain(s)* • ligai - *white* • i - *the one(s)*

White mountains. These high peaks are snow-covered much of the year. The range, though populated by the Ute, was hunting ground for the Navajo up until about 1895. They were eventually driven out by White dominance and by the hunting laws.

The San Juan River, Colorado, New Mexico, Utah: Tooh
The river. The San Juan originates in the San Juan Mountains (Dził Ligaii) of Colorado and flows into New Mexico and Utah, where it joins the Colorado River (Tó Nts'ósíkooh). The San Juan is also known as *Tooh Bikạ'í* (male river), *Nóóda'í Bitooh* (river of the Utes), and *Sạ́ Bitooh* (old age river).

San Mateo Peak, New Mexico: Tsoodził
tsoo' - *tongue* • dził - *mountain*

Tongue Mountain. See *Mount Taylor, New Mexico.*

San Mateo Range, New Mexico: Ghạ́ạ́' Deelzhah
ghạ́ạ́' - *top, summit, back* • deelzhah - *an undulating or jagged line*

A summit that is undulating or jagged in line. The San Mateo range, close to the northeast of Grants (Naatooh Sik'ai'í), is dominated by Mount Taylor (Tsoodził), whose near-summit timberline runs in a meandering or serpentine pattern, hence the Navajo name.

San Rafael, New Mexico: Tó Sido
tó - *water* • sido - *it is hot*

Hot water or hot springs. The village of San Rafael is 4 miles south of Grants (Naatooh Sik'ai'í) at the base of the eastern flanks of the Zuni Mountains. This was the site of old Fort Wingate.

Sand Springs, Arizona: Séi Bii' Tóhí
séi - *sand* • bii' - *in it* • tó - *water* • (h)í - *the place*

Where there is water or a spring in the sand. The site is about 20 miles north of Leupp (Tsiizizii) on Arizona Indian Highway 58.

Sanders, Arizona: Lichíí' Deez'áhí
lichíí' - *it is red* • deez'á - *it extends or lies as an elongated ridge or bluff* • (h)í - *the place, the one*

Extended red ridge or bluff. Sanders lies in red sandstone country some 42 miles west of Gallup (Na'nízhoozhí), New Mexico on the north bank of the Rio Puerco, off old Highway 66.

Sandia Mountains, New Mexico: Dził Náávisii
dził - *mountain* • náávisii - *turning, whirling*

Turning mountain. The name may refer to the fact that the mountain presents strikingly different faces and shapes when viewed from afar at slightly different angles. The Sandias rise to 10,600 feet at the crest. The deep canyons and gorges on the west face of the mountain were used by Navajos as points for raids on the Rio Grande River (Tooh Ba'áadii, Naakaii Bitooh) pueblos. The mountains loom closely to the east of Albuquerque (Bee'eldíildahsinil).

Sandia Pueblo, New Mexico: Kin Łigaai
kin - *house(s)* • łigai - *white, it is white* • í - *the one(s)*

White house or houses. This pueblo is on the east bank of the Rio Grande River (Tooh Ba'áadii, Naakaii Bitooh), 12 miles north of Albuquerque (Bee'eldíildahsinil). A number of sites in Navajo country (Diné Bikéyah) are named *Kin Łigaai*. See *Baca, New Mexico.*

Sanostee, New Mexico: Tsé Ałnáozt'i'í
tsé - *rock or rocks* • ałnáozt'i' - *they overlap* • í - *the place*

The place where rocks overlap or are layered. The name *Sanostee* is a non-Navajo rendition of *Tsé Ałnáozt'i'í*. This site is near the community proper of Sanostee, whose Navajo name is *Tóyaagai* (where white water rises), a reference which is descriptive of an extinct artesian well.

Santa Clara Pueblo, New Mexico: Naashashí
(a)naa' - *enemy, enemies* • shash - *bear* • í - *the one(s)*

Bear enemies, enemies like bears. Santa Clara is on the west bank of the Rio Grande River (Tooh Ba'áadii, Naakaii Bitooh), 25 miles north of Santa Fe (Yootó).

Santa Fe, New Mexico: Yootó
yoo' - *bead* • tó - *water*

Bead water. The Navajo name possibly refers to the Santa Fe Creek, from the Tewa Indian name. Santa Fe, in north-central New Mexico on the western slopes of the Santa Fe Mountains, is New Mexico's capital. It was founded between 1609 and 1610 by Don Pedro de Peralta. It is 60 miles north of Albuquerque (Bee'eldíildahsinil).

Santo Domingo Pueblo, New Mexico: Tóhajiiloh
tó - *water* • hajiiloh - *they pull it up with a rope*

They pull water up with a rope. This pueblo is 30 miles southwest of Santa Fe (Yootó). Don Juan de Onate reportedly named it as he did it because he arrived at the place on Sunday, *domingo.*

Satan Pass, New Mexico: Hahodeeshtł'izhí
ha - *up, upward* • ho - *space, area* • deeshtł'izh - *blue extends along* • í - *the place*

The place where blue extends along upward. This deep canyon pass leads from near Thoreau (Dłǫ́'áyázhí) to Crownpoint (T'iists'óóz Ndeeshgizh). The pass is 14 miles north of Thoreau.

Sawmill, Arizona: Ni'iijíhí
ni'iijííh - *crosswise sawing is done* • í - *the place*

The place where crosswise sawing is done. The reference is to either of the two sawmills north of Fort Defiance (Tséhootsooí), although the older one is often more specifically called *Ni'iijííh Hasání* (old sawmill). The newer mill is located at Red Lake (Be'ek'id Halchíí'), 23 miles north of Window Rock (Tséghahoodzání). The old mill is 19 miles north of Fort Defiance.

Segi Canyon, Arizona: Tséyi'
tsé - *rock(s)* • yi' - *in, within*

Within the rocks. This Navajo name is a general term for large canyons, Canyon de Chelly, for example. Segi Canyon is 11 miles southwest of Kayenta (Tó Dínéeshzhee'). The canyon and its side canyons contain numerous Anasazi ruins.

Segihotsosi Canyon, Arizona: Tséyi' Hats'ózí
tsé - *rock(s)* • yi' - *in, within* • tséyi' - *canyon* • ha - *area, space* • ts'óz - *narrow, slender, slim* • í - *the one*

Narrow within the rocks, narrow canyon. This deep canyon is in the Monument Valley (Tsé Bii' Ndzisgaii) area.

Seven Lakes, New Mexico: Tsosts'id Be'ek'id
tsosts'id - *seven* • be'ek'id - *lake or lakes*

Literally seven lakes. These ephemeral lakes were in the desert some 17 miles northeast of Crownpoint (T'iists'óóz Ńdeeshgizh). There is now only one lake in the area and it is dry most of the time.

Shabikeshchee Village, New Mexico: Shá Bik'e'eshchí
shá - *the sun* • bi - *it* • k'e (k'i) - *on, upon* • 'eshchį - *it is written or carved*

The sun is written or carved upon it. This basketmaker ruin in Chaco Canyon (Tsé Bíyah Anii'áhí) is about one mile soustheast of Wijiji (Díwózhiishzhiin). A large sun is carved into a stone near the site. This location is also called *Tsé Bik'e'eshchį* (rock with carving upon it).

Shalimar Lounge, Gallup, New Mexico: Dah Njiilsaadí
dah - *up, elevated* • njiilsaad - *seated with an expectant or anxious demeanor* • í - *the place*

The place where people are seated up (on bar stools) anxiously or expectantly looking for a pickup or a date. The inn and lounge are on old Highway 66 in Gallup (Na'nízhoozhí).

Sheep Hill, Arizona: Dibé Dah Shijé'é
dibé - *sheep* • dah - *up, up at an elevation* • shijé'é - *they lie*

Sheep lie up at an elevation. The pine-covered hill is 6 miles east of Flagstaff (Kin Łání). There are 13th century Anasazi ruins nearby.

Sheep Manure Spring, Arizona: Dibé Bichaan Bii' Tó
dibé - *sheep* • bi - *his, her, its, their* • chaan (chąą') - *manure* • bii' - *in it* • tó - *water, spring*

Spring in the sheep manure. This spring is 27 miles north of Many Farms (Dá'ák'eh Halání) and about 20 miles southwest of Rock Point (Tsé Lichíí' Deez'áhí, Tsé Ntsaa Deez'áhí).

Sheep Springs, New Mexico: **Tooh Haltsooí**
tooh - *river, stream, body of water* • haltso - *an area is yellow or light green*
í - *the place*
A meadow where there is water or a spring. Sheep Springs is 47 miles north of
Gallup (Na'nízhoozhí). The Navajos also call this place simply *Haltsooí* (place of
the meadow or meadows).

Shipaulovi, Arizona: **Tsétsohk'id**
tsé - *rock* • tsoh - *big* • k'id - *hill*
Hill of the big rock. This Hopi village is situated on Second Mesa north of
Mishongnovi. The Navajo name also refers to the villages of Mishongnovi and
Toreva. The eastern area of the Hopi Villages begins 11 miles west of Keams Ca-
nyon (Lók'a'deeshjin).

Shiprock, New Mexico: **Naat'áanii Nééz**
naat'áanii - *leader, chief, boss* • nééz - *tall*
Tall leader or boss. The term refers to Superintedent William T. Shelton, who
originated the San Juan School in 1903 for the northern Navajos, and who was
responsible for much economic as well as educational progress in the area. Shiprock
community is also called *Toohdi* (at the river), alluding to the proximity to the
San Juan River (Tooh, Tooh Bikạ'í, Nóóda'í Bitooh, Sạ Bitooh). Shiprock is 27
miles west of Farmington (Tóta').

Shiprock Pinnacle, New Mexico: **Tsé Bit'a'í**
tsé - *rock* • bi - *his, her, its* • t'a' - *wing* • í - *the one*
Rock with wings, winged rock. This mammoth volcanic structure in northwest
New Mexico has, from some angles, the appearance of possessing wings. The rock
stands at 7,178 feet in the desert about 12 miles southwest of Shiprock Community
(Naat'áanii Nééz, Toohdi).

Shonto, Arizona: **Shạạ́'tóhí**
shạạ́' - *sunshine, in the sun, on the sunny side* • tó - *water* • (h)í - *the place,*
the one
Where the spring is in the sun or on the sunny side. This is also the name for Sunrise
Spring, Arizona. Shonto is 30 miles east of Kaibito (K'ai' Bii' Tó).

Shungopavi, Arizona: **Kin Názt'i'**
kin - *house(s), building(s)* • názt'i' - *lying in he form of a circle, encircling*
Houses in a circle. This Hopi village is on the point of the southwest projection
of Second Mesa. The eastern part of the Hopi Villages begins 11 miles west of
Keams Canyon (Lók'a'deeshjin).

Sichomovi, Arizona: **Ayahkin**
ayah - *underneath, below* • kin - *house(s), building(s)*
House or houses below. This Hopi village is atop First Mesa between Walpi
(Deez'áajị') and Hano (Naashashí). The Navajo name alludes, as it does in one of
the general terms for the Hopi Villages (Ayahkinii), to underground kivas.

Sierra Blanca Peak, Colorado: **Sis Naajiní, Tsis Naajiní**
sis (tsis) - *mountain* • naa - *around, across* • jin - *black* • í - *the one*

Mountain with black around it, belted with black. When the peak is snow covered the dark forested area between the snow and the lighter colored lower portion of the mountain forms a dark band across the breadth of the mountain, giving it a belted appearance. The term *black belted mountain* might also be appropriate because the Navajo word *sis* means *belt* as well as *mountain*. Blanca Peak, as it is also called, rises to over 14,000 feet 20 miles east of Alamosa, Colorado. It is considered to be the sacred mountain of the east of Navajo mythology. The mountain is known ceremonially as *Jóhonaa'éí Dziil* (Sun Mountain) and *Yoołgai Dziil* (White Shell Mountain).

Shiprock Pinnacle, New Mexico: Tsé Bit'a'í

Sitting Pig, New Mexico: Bisóodi Sidáhí
bisóodi - *pig, hog* • sidá - *it sits* • (h)í - *the place*
Where the pig sits. This small swine-shaped sandstone formation is east of Asaayi Lake (Asaayi') on the western slopes of the Chuska Mountains (Ch'óshgai).

Sleeping Ute Mountain, Colorado: Dził Naajiní
dził - *mountain* • naa - *downward, down* • jin - *black* • í - *the one*
The mountain that is black downward. This mountain 15 miles southwest of Cortez (Tséyaatóhí) resembles, from certain angles, a reclining or sleeping person. The Navajo name describes only its black streak characteristic. The component *naa* in the Navajo word *naajin* above can mean *across* or *vertically down*. Both concepts are widely used in Navajo place names. See *Sierra Blanca Peak, Colorado,* above.

Sliding House, Arizona: Kin Náázhoozhí
kin - *house, building* • náázhoozh - *it slid down* • í - *the one*

The house that slid down. This 12th ccentury Anasazi ruin is on the north side of Canyon de Chelly (Tséyi'), about 3 miles north of White House Ruin (Kiníí' Na'ígai).

Small Canyon, New Mexico: Tsékooh Yázhí
tsékooh - *rock canyon* • yázhí - *small*

Small rock canyon. This canyon is behind Casa Rinconada (Kin Názbąs) in Chaco Canyon (Tsé Bíyah Anii'áhí). Chaco Canyon is 35 miles north of Crownpoint (T'iists'óóz Ńdeeshgizh).

Smith Lake, New Mexico: Tsin Názbąs
tsin - *tree(s), pole(s)* • názbąs - *a circle*

A circle of trees or poles. This sometime lake is situated about 10 miles north of Thoreau (Dlǫ́'áyázhí), on the road to Crownpoint (T'iists'óóz Ńdeeshgizh).

Smoke Signal, Arizona: Łid Néigahí
łid - *smoke* • néi - *repeatedly, again* • gah (gaii) - *white* • í - *the place, the one*

Where there is repeated white smoke. White smoke that appears again and again. The origin of this name is uncertain. Smoke Signal is 30 miles west of Chinle (Ch'ínílí).

Snowflake, Arizona: Tó Diłhił Biih Yílį
tó - *water, spring* • diłhił - *it is dark* • biih - *into it* • yílí - *it flows*

Where it flows into dark water. Snowflake is 28 miles south of Holbrook (T'iisyaakin) on the east bank of Silver Creek. The village was used by the Navajos in the late 1800's as a stopping and trading place on their way to trade in White Mountain Apache country.

Socorro, New Mexico: Sighóla
sighóla - *a Navajo rendition of Spanish socorro* (help, succor)

The area near Socorro was frequently raided by the Navajos. This community is situated on the Rio Grande River (Tooh Ba'áadii, Naakaii Bitooh) about 75 miles south of Albuquerque (Bee'eldííldahsinil).

Sonsela Buttes, Arizona: Sǫ' Silá
sǫ' - *star, stars* • silá - *they sit (as a pair)*

A pair of sitting stars. The reference is to the two volcanic buttes, sacred to the Navajos, situated about 5 miles northwest of Crystal (Tó Niłts'ílí), New Mexico. Chee Dodge, the last chief of the Navajos, and called by them *Hastiin Adiits'a'ii* (Mr. Interpreter), lived and ranched in the territory south of Sǫ' Silá.

Squirrel Springs, New Mexico: Dlodziłgaii Bito'
dlo (dlǫ́ǫ́') - *prairie dog* • dził - *mountain* • gaii - *white* • dlodziłgaii - *squirrel* • bi - *his, her, its* • to' - *water, spring*

Squirrel water, squirrel spring. The spring is 5 miles east of Windy Canyon (Tsé Bii' Naayolí), near the head of Mexican Springs (Naakaii Bito') wash.

Standing Rock, New Mexico: Tsé Íí'áhí
tsé - *rock* • íí'á - *at points or extends upward* • (h)í - *the one*

Rock that points upward. This pinnacle is about 14 miles east of Coyote Canyon (Mą'ii Tééh Yítłizhí). There is a trading post and day school at the site. The Navajo name is also the term for Churchrock Spires and the Four Corners region. The name is generally used to describe any upright crag or aiguille.

Star Lake, New Mexico: Chéch'il Dah Łichíí'

ché (tsé) - *rock* • ch'il - *plant* • chéch'il - *oak tree(s)* • dah - *up, elevated* łichíí' - *red*

Red oak up at an elevation. Star Lake is in barren desert and mesa country 55 miles northeast of Crownpoint (T'iists'óóz Ńdeeshgizh).

Steamboat Canyon, Arizona: Tóyéé'

tó - *water* • yéé' - *scarce*

Scarce water. This small canyon is about 25 miles east of Keams Canyon (Lók'a'deeshjin). There are Anasazi ruins in the area, and Navajo and Hopi petroglyphs on the sandstone walls of the canyon.

Stepped Rock Trail, Arizona: Tsé Hadeesk'įh

tsé - *rock* • ha - *up out* • deesk'įh - *layered*

Layered or overlapping rock up out. This horse trail, a couple of miles up Canyon del Muerto (Ane'é Tséyi'), has steps made of overlapping stones.

Stinking Lake, New Mexico: Tó Ndoots'osí

tó - *water* • ndoots'os - *long and narrow* • í - *the one*

Long narrow water. The lake is known as one of the traditional stopping places of the Navajo *Tábąąhá* (Water's Edge) clan on their journey west from the Rio Grande and Gallinas valleys. This tarn is situated in the high mesa country of the Jicarilla Apache Reservation, some 30 miles north of Cuba (Na'azísí To'í), New Mexico.

St. Johns, Arizona: Tsézhin Deez'áhí

tsé - *rock* • zhin - *black* • tsézhin - *lava* • deez'á - *it extends as a ridge or bluff, or is pointed* • (h)í - *the one*

Lava extending as a ridge, or a lava point. Situated 53 miles south of Sanders (Łichíí' Deez'áhí), this Mormon farming and ranching town was once an active location for Navajo trading.

St. Michaels, Arizona: Ts'íhootso

ts'í - *extending out horizontally* • hoo - *area, space* • tso - *yellow, greenish* hootso - *meadow, pasture*

A greenish area, or meadow, extends out horizontally. Situated above verdant meadows about 3 miles west of Window Rock (Tségháhoodzání), St. Michaels is the site of a Franciscan mission. It was the home of the late Father Berard Haile, missionary to the Navajos, famed linguist, and student of, as well as writer about, the Navajo language.

Stoney Butte, New Mexico: Tséłgaii

tsé - *rock* • łgai (łigai) - *it is white* • í - *the one*

White rock. This large rocky mesa is located about 20 miles in the desert north of Crownpoint (T'iists'óóz Ndeeshgizh). The Navajo name is common for many areas containing whitish rock.

Suanee, New Mexico: K'aalógii Dziil

k'aalógii - *butterfly* • dziil - *mountain*

Butterfly mountain. The Navajo name is derived from a barren mountain 3 miles south of Suanee, one of the mesas from which the Navajos are reputed to gather their sacred mirage stone. This was also the site of a trading post and store on old U.S. Highway 66. Suanee is about 30 miles southwest of Albuquerque (Bee'eldíildahsinil).

Sulphur Springs, New Mexico: Séí Ha'atiin

séí - *sand* • ha - *up out* • 'atiin - *trail, road, path*

Sandy road or trail up out. This spring, the site of an old Navajo resting and camping place, is east of the Tunicha Range (Tó Ntsaa) and about 4 miles north of Newcomb (Bis Deez'áhí).

Sunrise, Arizona: Séí Ńdeeshgizh

séí - *sand* • ńdeeshgizh - *gap, cut*

Sand gap. This location is about 30 miles northwest of Winslow (Béésh Sinil), near Leupp (Tsiizizii).

Sunrise Spring, Arizona: Shąą'tóhí

shąą' - *sunshine, on the sunny side* • tó - *water, spring* • (h)í - *the place, the one*

Where there is water or a spring on the sunny side. Sunrise Spring is 10 miles southwest of Ganado (Lók'aahnteel) on Arizona Highway 15. The Navajo name *Shąą'tóhí* is also given to Shonto, Arizona.

Sunset Crater, Arizona: Dził Bilátah Łitsooí
dził - *mountain* • bí - *its* • látah - *tip* • łitso(o) - *it is yellow* •
i - *the one*

Yellow-tipped mountain. Sunset Crater, with its brownish red cast gives the crater a golden, sunset-like luster. The crater is 16 miles north of Flagstaff (Kin Łání) and about 6 miles east of San Francisco Peak (Dook'o'oosłíid).

Sweetwater, Arizona: Tó Łikan
tó - *water, spring* • łikan - *it is sweet*

Sweet water. The location is 15 miles northeast of Rock Point (Tsé Łichíí' Deez'áhí, Tsé Ntsaa Deez'áhí) on the south side of the Keet Seel (Kits'iiłí) wash. No Water Mesa (Tó Ádin Dah Azką́) lies closely to the north.

T&R Market (near Gallup), New Mexico: Ts'ah Bii' Ch'iyáán Bá Hooghan
ts'ah - *sagebrush (Artemesia tridentata)* • bii' - *in it* • ch'iyáán - *food*
bá - *for him, her, it* • hooghan - *home* • ch'iyáán bá hooghan - *food store, market*

Food store in the sagebrush. Also called *Ałk'i Dah Yiłk'idí* (where hills are on top of hills), this market handles groceries, hay, firewood, gasoline, pawn and other goods. It is owned by renowned local tennis doubles ace, Colin Tanner, called by the Navajos *Shash Yáázh Bináłí* (Grandson of Little Bear). The complex is 5 miles north of Gallup (Na'nízhoozhí) on U.S. Highway 666. It has a large Navajo clientele.

Tanner Spring, Arizona: K'ai' Si'ání
k'ai' - *willow(s) (Salix fluviatilis)* • si'ą́ - *it sits in position* • (n)í - *the place*

Where there is a lone willow, or possibly a cluster of willows. This spot is in the Wide Ruins (Kinteel) area, northwest of Chambers (Ch'ilzhoo'). In 1884 there was fighting between Navajos and Whites at Tanner Spring over land and water possession.

Taos, New Mexico: Tówoł
tó - *water, spring* • woł - *the gurgling sound of a stream*

The sound of water. A stream runs through the center of this beautiful pueblo. In 1540 the pueblo was visited by Hernando de Alvarado, a member of Coronado's conquistadores. Taos is 74 miles north of Santa Fe (Yootó).

Taylor Spring, Arizona: Asdzáni Taah Yíyá
asdzáni - *a young woman* • taah - *into the water* • yiyá - *she went*

Where a young woman went into the water. Taylor Spring is less than 2 miles west of Chambers (Ch'ilzhóó').

Teec Nos Pos, Arizona: T'iis Názbąs
t'iis - *cottonwood tree(s)* • názbąs - *circle, circular*

Cottonwoods in a circle. This site is near Four Corners (Tsé Íí'áhí) and close to the base of the northern slopes of the Carrizo Mountains (Dził Náhooziłii).

Tesuque Pueblo, New Mexico: Tł'oh Łikizhí
tł'oh - *grass* • łikizh - *it is spotted* • í - *the place*

Where the grass is spotted. The Pueblo Rebellion of 1680 began here. This Tewa-speaking pueblo is 6 miles north of Santa Fe.

The Gap, Arizona: Tsinaabąąs Habitiin

tsin - *wood* • naabąąs - *it rolls about* • tsinaabąąs - *a wagon*

A wagon trail up and out. See *Coppermine, Arizona.*

Thohedlih, New Mexico: Tó Aheedlį

tó - *water(s)* • ahee (ahi) - *convergent* • (d)lį - *flow*

Waters converge, flow together. This site is near the confluence of the San Juan (Tooh, Tooh Bikạ'í, Nóóda'í Bitooh, Sạ́ Bitooh) and the Los Pinos Rivers in northern New Mexico, near Navajo State Park. In Navajo legend it is the source of the *Tó Aheedlíinii* (Waters-Flow-Together) clan.

Thoreau, New Mexico: Dlǫ́'áyázhí

dlǫ́' (dlǫ́ǫ́) - *prairie dog* • (á)yázhí - *little small*

Little prairie dog. The Navajo name was the sobriquet of a trader and merchant in the area. There is, coincidentally, a large prairie dog population in the region. Thoreau achieved some prominence as a commercial Navajo silversmithing center. It is 30 miles east of Gallup (Na'nízhoozhí), just off U.S. I-40.

Three-Turkey House, Arizona: Tsénii'kiní

tsé - *rock* • nii' - *niche, nostril* • kin - *house, building* • i - *the one, the place*

House in a rock niche. This cliff dwelling is about 20 miles southeast of Chinle (Ch'ínílį) in Three-Turkey House Canyon (Chíihłigai). It is also known as *Tạzhii Bikin* (turkey's house). Three red and white turkeys were painted on the walls of one of the houses in the ruin.

Three-Turkey House, Arizona: Tsénii'kiní

Three-Turkey House Canyon, Arizona: Chííhłigai
chííh - *red ochre* • łigai - *it is white*
White ochre. The canyon contains Three-Turkey House (Tsénii'kini). See *Three-Turkey House, Arizona,* above.

Tierra Amarilla, New Mexico: Łitsooí
łitso(o) - *it is yellow, yellow earth* • í - *the place*
Where the earth is yellow. Yellowish clay deposits in the area are the genesis for both the Spanish and the Navajo names.The village is 49 miles north of Abiquiu (Ha'ashgizh), in the Chama River valley.

Toadlena, New Mexico: Tó Háálį́
tó - *water, spring* • há(á) - *up and out* • łį - *it flows*
It flows up and out. This is an old Navajo name for the site. The present community is situated on the eastern flank of the Tunicha range (Tóntsaa), from which flow many springs. Toadlena is 79 miles north of Gallup (Na'nízboozhí) and 12 miles west of Newcomb (Bis Deez'áhí). A boarding school was established here in 1911.

Todilto, New Mexico: Tó Dildǫ'
tó - *water, spring* • dildǫ' - *it pops, explodes*
Water that pops. Sounding water. The reference is possibly to water falling and striking stone. This spring is on the west side of the Chuska Mountains (Ch'óshgai), northeast of Red Lake (Be'ek'id Halchíí'), which is the receptacle for the waters flowing from this spring.

Todokozh Spring, Arizona: Tó Dík'ǫ́ǫ́zhí
tó - *water* • dík'ǫ́ǫ́zh - *salty, sour, bitter* í - *the one*
Sour water. This alkaline spring is northeast of Salahkai Mesa (Tséligai) in Apache County.

Tohatchi, New Mexico: Tóhaach'i'
tó - *water, spring* • haach'i' - *it is scratched out*
Water is scratched out. The creek bed running down to Tohatchi from the south side of the Chuska Mountains (Ch'óshgai) is sandy in places, permitting water to be uncovered by digging with the hands. Tohatchi is 25 miles north of Gallup (Na'nízhoozhí).

Tohatchi Pass, New Mexico: Bighá'iígeedí
bighá - *through it* • 'iígeed - *a cut-through gap or pass* • í - *the place*
The place where a gap or pass is cut through. This spot is just east of Tohatchi (Tóhaach'i'). It serves as a pass for U.S. Highway 666.

Tolakai, New Mexico: Tó Łigaai Háálíni
tó - *water, spring* • łigaai - *white, white one* • há(á) - *up and out* • łį - *it flows* • (n)í - *the place*
The place where white water flows up and out. This site, 9 miles north of Gallup (Na'nízhoozhí), derives its name from whitish water flowing up behind the old trading post just off U.S. Highway 666.

61

Tolani Lakes, Arizona: Tó Łání
tó - *water* • łání - *many, much*
Much water, many bodies of water. These small lakes are about 15 miles northeast of Leupp (Tsiizizii), on the way to Oraibi (Oozéí). This is also the name for Laguna, New Mexico.

Tolcheco, Arizona: Tółchí'íkooh
tó - *water, spring* • łchí'í (łichíí') - *red* • kooh - *wash, arroyo*
Red water wash. This is the site of a former trading post and mission situated 15 miles northwest of Leupp (Tsiizizii) in the bottom of the Little Colorado River, which some Navajos also call *Tółchí'íkooh.*

Tonalea, Arizona: Tó Nehelį́į́h
tó - *water, spring* • nehe (nihi) - *as far as, to a point* • lį́į́h (lį́) - *flow, it flows*
Water flows to a point (and forms a pond or lake). Now a storage dam, this place is 22 miles northeast of Tuba City (Tó Naneesdizí).

Toreva, Arizona: Tsétsohk'id
tsé - *rock* • tsoh - *big* • k'id - *hill*
Big rock hill. This Hopi village is at the southwest base of Second Mesa, below Mishongnovi, called by the same name by the Navajos. The Hopi Villages (Ayahkinii, Oozéí) are a few miles west of Keams Canyon (Lók'a'deeshjin).

Torreon, New Mexico: Ya'niilzhiin
ya (ya) - *sky* • niil - *extension to a point* • zhiin (zhin) - *black, dark*
Something dark or black at a distance in the sky (horizon implied, possibly). Navajos who live in, or have lived in Torreon, say that this name refers to the distant Cabezon Butte (Tsé Naajiin), 20 miles or so to the southeast, which they can see from Torreon. It is also called *Dolión,* a Navajo rendition of *Torreon.*

Towaoc, Colorado: Kin Dootł'izhí
kin - *house, building* • dootł'izh - *blue or green* • í - *the one*
Blue or green house. This Ute settlement with boarding school is 30 miles northwest of Shiprock (Naat'áanii Nééz, Toohdi), New Mexico, on the eastern slopes of Sleeping Ute Mountain (Dził Naajiní).

Towayaalane Mesa, New Mexico: Tséé'dóhdoon
tséé' (tséii) - *in the rock* • dóhdoon - *it rumbles*
A rumbling in the rock. The interpretation of this Navajo name is possibly related to Zuni mythology, which considers the sacred mesa to be a place where thunder, lightning and rain are created. A current non-Zuni name for the mesa is *Thunder Mountain.* However, the Zuni meaning of the name *Towayaalane* is *Corn Mountain.* This magnificent butte lies a short distance to the southeast of Zuni Pueblo (Naasht'ézhí) and immediately southwest of Blackrock (Tsézhįįh Deezlį́, Chézhįįh Deezlį́). An alternative spelling of the Zuni name is *Dowa Yalanne.*

Towering House, New Mexico: Kin Yaa'á
kin - *house, building* • yaa'á - *it sticks up, extends upward*
House that stands up. This ruin near Crownpoint (T'iists'óóz Ńdeeshgizh) was built centuries ago by the Anasazi. Ancestors of the Navajo came into the area and became known as *Kiyaa'áanii (Kinyaa'áanii),* the Towering House clan.

The walls of this structure still stand in the desert in the Crownpoint Borrego Pass (Dibé Yázhí Habitiin) region.

Trail The Mexicans Came Down, Arizona: Naakaii Adáánání

naakaii - *Mexican(s)* • adáá (ada, adah) - *down from a height* • ná - *move, migrate* • (n)í - *the place*

The place where the Mexicans came down. This horse trail is in Canyon del Muerto (Ane'é Tséyi'). The trail was used in 1805 by Lieutenant Chacon to attack Massacre Cave with a division of troops. The trail is also called *Naakaii Bidáánání (same meaning)* and *Naakaii Habitiin* (Mexican trail up and out).

Trail Where The Enemy Walked Up Singing, Arizona: Anaa' Sin Yił Haayáhí

anaa' - *enemy* • sin - *song* • yił - *with him, her, it* • haa - *up and out* yá - *he, she, it goes* • (h)í - *the place*

Where the enemy walked up and out with a song. A horse trail, this place is a couple of miles up Canyon de Chelly (Tséyi'). The Utes reputedly used the trail for raids into the canyon in the 1840's.

Tsaile, Arizona: Tsééhílį

tsééh - *into rock, into a canyon* • (y)ílį - *it flows*

It flows into a canyon. The name refers to the place where Tsaile Creek enters the head of Canyon del Muerto (Ane'é Tséyi') southwest of Tsaile Butte (Tsézhin Sizíní). Tsaile is some 55 miles north of Window Rock (Tségháhoodzání). It is the home of Navajo Community College (Diné Bi'ólta' Wódahgoigíí).

Tsaile Butte, Arizona: Tsézhin Sizíní

tsé - *rock* • zhin - *black* • tsézhin - *lava* • sizį - *it stands, is standing* (n)í - *the one*

Standing black rock, standing lava. This steep igneous pinnacle, sacred to the Navajos, rises southeast of Navajo Community College (Diné Bi'ólta' Wódahgoigíí) at Tsaile (Tsééhílį).

Tsaya, New Mexico: Tséyaa

tsé - *rock* • yaa - *beneath, under*

Beneath the rock. A trading post was situated here some 12 miles northeast of Chaco Canyon (Tsé Bíyah Anii'áhí). Tsaya Canyon is one of the major tributaries into Chaco Canyon from the north.

Tse Bonito, Arizona: Tsé Binii' Tó

tsé - *rock* • bi - *his, her, its* • (a)nii' - *face* • tó - *water*

Rock-face water. Water on the face of the rock. The words *binii' tó* have been incorrectly rendered as *bonito*, (Spanish for *pretty, beautiful*) by non-Navajos, creating the misconception that the name is made up of a both a Navajo and a Spanish word. The Navajo term, glossed as above, proves it otherwise. The rock, near Window Rock (Tségháhoodzání) and the Haystacks (Tséta' Ch'ééch'i), seeps water from an interior spring. It was an overnight stopping place for Navajos under captivity to, and being moved by, U.S. troops from Fort Defiance (Tséhootsooí) to Fort Sumner (Hwéeldi) during the Long Walk.

Tsedaatah Canyon, New Mexico: Tsédáá'tah

tsé - *rock* • dáá' - *rim, edge* • tah - *among*

Among the rock edges or rims. Tsedaatah Canyon is about 15 miles west of Lukachukai (Lók'a'ch'égai). The area contains Anasazi ruins. During the Navajo wars of of 1864 the Navajos hid out in this canyon.

Tseda Hwidezohi Peak, Arizona: Tsédáá' Hwiidzohí
tsé - *rock* • dáá' - *edge, rim* • hwii (ho) - *space, area* • dzoh - *draw a line or mark* • í - *the place*

The place where there is a mark or line, or marks or lines, carved into the edge of the rock. The peak is on the east rim of Black Mesa (Dziłíjiin), above Rough Rock (Tséch'izhí).

Tsehso, New Mexico: Tsétsoh
tsé - *rock* • tsoh - *big*

Big rock. This is a Chaco Canyon (Tsé Bíyah Anii'áhí) site of an Anasazi ruin containing 4 Kivas and 24 rooms.

Tsin Sikaad, Arizona: Tsin Sikaad
tsin - *tree, wood* • sikaad - *it sits, they sit in clumps*

Sitting tree or trees. Clumps or bunches of trees. This site is some 15 miles north of Chinle (Ch'ínílí).

Tuba City, Arizona: Tó Naneesdizí
tó - *water, spring* • nanee (nani) - *around about* • (s)diz - *it is twisted* • í - *the place*

Where water winds about or twists about. Haile calls it *tangled water.* There is ground seepage in the area today. The name might also refer to irrigation ditches used by earlier Mormon settlers. The community is 26 miles northeast of Cameron (Na'ní'á Hayázhí). There are dinosaur tracks in nearby sandstone formations.

Tunicha Mountains, Arizona and New Mexico: Tóntsaa
tó - *water* • ntsaa - *big*

Big water. The name refers to the numerous lakes on the range. The Tunicha Mountains are part of a mountain chain running from southeast to northwest in northern New Mexico and Arizona. The southeastern part of the range is called *Ch'óshgai* (white spruce), the central part *Tó Ntsaa* (big water) and the northern area *Lók'a'ch'égai* (reeds extending out white).

Tunnel Spring, Arizona: Tséníí'tóhí
tsé - *rock* • níí' - *niche* • tó - *water, spring* • (h)í - *the place*

The place where there is a spring in the crevice of a rock. This spring is in a niche in sandstone formation about 5 miles north of Fort Defiance (Tséhootsooí). There are many carvings of names in this recess, the earliest being 1878.

Turley, New Mexico: Náshdóí Bighan
náshdóí - *wildcat* • bighan - *his, her, its, home, house*

Wildcat's house. According to Van Valkenburgh, the Navajo name refers to a heavily moustached former inhabitant. The village is on the banks of the San Juan River (Tooh, Tooh Biką'í, Nóóda'í Bitooh, Sá Bitooh) eight miles upstream from Blanco (Taahóóteel).

Tuye Spring, New Mexico: Tóyéé'
tó - *water* • yéé' - *scarce*

Scarce water. This also the name for Steamboat Canyon, Arizona. The site is 15 miles southeast of Tohatchi (Tóhaach'i'). In bygone days this area was an important Navajo gathering place. Mud springs and alkaline water prevail at the spot. The first known trading post was established here in 1892.

Twin Buttes, (near Gallup), New Mexico: Tsézhin Sinil
tsé - *rock* • zhin - *black* • tsézhin - *lava* • sinil - *they sit, they lie*

Sitting black rock or lava. These once prominent peaks a couple of miles west of Gallup (Na'nízhoozhí) have been ravaged by a paving construction company. Many Navajos live in the area.

Twin Lakes, New Mexico: Tsénáhádzoh
tsé - *rock(s)* • ná - *circular shape* • há - *space, area* • dzoh - *to draw a mark, establish a boundary*

An area bounded by a circle of rocks. There are two ephemeral shallow lakes and a day school at this site 11 miles north of Gallup (Na'nízhoozhí). An earlier government school was built near the lakes in the 1930's by Niram A. Wilson and crew. The building no longer exists. Another name for the Twin Lakes area is *Báhástł'ah* (inside corner, recess). Haile says that this name designates a cove or recess where Highway 666 descends into the Twin Lakes valley and Tohatchi (Tóhaach'i') watersheds. Many old Navajo sites are in the area, which is still thickly populated by the members of the tribe.

Two Gray Hills, New Mexico: Bis Dah Łitso
bis - *clay, adobe* • dah - *up, at an elevation* • łitso - *yellow*

Upper yellow clay. The term is a reference to the hilly, yellowish-colored earth in the area. Two Gray Hills rugs are among the finest produced on the reservation. The site is 10 miles west of Newcomb (Bis Deez'áhí) on the eastern slopes of the Tunicha Range (Tó Ntsaa).

Two Wells, New Mexico: K'ai' Ńt'i'í
k'ai' - *willows* • ńt'i' - *they extend in a line* • í - *the place*

Where willows extend in a line. Two wells is 23 miles south of Gallup (Na'nízhoozhí) and about 10 miles east of Jones Ranch (Jééhkał).

Tyende Mesa, Arizona: Téé'ndééh
téé (tééh) - *into the water* • ndééh ('andééh) - *things fall*

Things fall into the water. Reference is to nearby Tyende Creek into which animals fall. This red sandstone mesa is near Kayenta (Tó Dínéeshzhee').

Walpi, Arizona: Deez'áají'
deez'á - *it lies or extends (a ridge or a mesa)* • jį' - *up to a point or the point*

It extends up to a point. This Hopi village is on the extreme point or tip of East or First Mesa. The present site dates from 1680, the time of the Pueblo Revolt. The villages begin a few miles west of Keams Canyon (Lók'a'deeshjin).

Washington Pass, New Mexico: Béésh Łichíi'ii Bigiizh
béésh - *metal, flint* • łichíi' - *it is red* • béésh łichíi' - *copper* • ii - *the one, the place* • bigiizh - *a cut or gap*

Red metal gap, copper gap. There are metallic formations in the pass. It is named after Lieutenant Colonel John Washington, who, in an expedition against the Navajos in 1849, passed through this gap. The pass is traversed now on a paved highway cutting through the Chuska Mountains (Ch'óshgai), from Sheep Springs (Tooh Haltsooí) on the eastern side, to Crystal (Tó Niłts'ilí) on the western slopes.

Waterflow, New Mexico: Ch'įįdiiłchíí'

ch'įįdii - *ghost, devil, evil spirit* • łichíí' - *red, it is red*

Red devil. This sobriquet is said to refer to a former trader at the community. The Navajo word *łichíí'* can also mean *he or she is naked*. The village is 15 miles east of Shiprock (Naat'áanii Nééz) on the north bank of the San Juan River (Tooh, Tooh Biką'í, Nóóda'í Bitooh, Są Bitooh).

West Maloney and Old 666 Junction, (Gallup), New Mexico: Tsé Naanáz'áhí

tsé - *rock (here, pavement)* • naanáz'á - *a curve* • (h)í - *the place*

Where the pavement makes a curve. This junction in northwest Gallup was the main route out of town onto old Highway 666 northward to Shiprock (Toohdi, Naat'áanii Nééz) and Farmington (Tóta').

Wheatfields Lake, Arizona: Tó Dzís'á

tó - *water* • dzí(s) - *away into space or into the distance* • 'á - *it extends*

Water that extends away into the distance. This beautiful lake reaches from its west bank, near Highway 12, toward the east where it meets the western slope of the Chuska Mountains (Ch'óshgai). The lake is about 10 miles southeast of Tsaile (Tsééhílí).

Wheatfields Lake, Arizona: Tó Dzís'á

Wheatfields Canyon, Arizona: Nát'ostse' Ál'íní

nát'oh - *tobacco* • tse' (tsé) - *stone, rock* • nát'ostse' - *pipe or pipes* •
ál'į́ - *it, or they, are made* • (n)í - *the place*

The place where tobacco stones (stone pipes) are made. Haile reports that pipes
were made of lava, some of them somewhat like modern cigarette holders, others
with bowl and stem. Both are depicted on sandpaintings. Wheatfields Canyon is
at the northern end of Canyon de Chelly about 10 miles southeast of Tsaile
(Tsééhílį́).

Where The Mexicans Cried, Arizona: Naakaii Deíchahí

naakaii - *Mexican(s)* • deícha (dayícha) - *they cried, wept* • (h)í - *the place*

The place where the Mexicans cried. The origin of this Navajo name has three
versions. The first version, and the most frequent, relates that many years ago
a group of Mexicans hauling freight in a wagon bogged down in sand about 5 miles
east of Ganado (Lók'aahnteel), worked for many hours wihout succeeding in get-
ting out, and so wept. Another rendition is that, after becoming stuck in the sand,
the group was ambushed by Navajos, whereupon they cried for mercy. The third
account tells that the Mexicans, while resting that night after a day of futile labor,
broke out their guitars and sang *mariachi* songs, which the Navajos wryly inter-
preted as weeping.

Whip-Poor-Will, Arizona: Séí Bii' Tóhí

séí - *sand* • bii' - *in it* • tó - *water, spring* • (h)í - *the place*

Where there is a spring in the sand. See *Sand Springs, Arizona*, which is another
name for *Whip-Poor-Will, Arizona*.

Whiskey Creek, Arizona, New Mexico: Tódiłhił

tó - *water, spring* • diłhił - *it is dark*

Dark water. This is also the word for whiskey. The origin of Whiskey Creek is
in the Tunicha Range (Tó Ntsaa). It empties into Canyon de Chelly (Tséyi') about
15 miles north of Navajo (Ni'iijíhí), New Mexico.

Whiskey Lake, New Mexico: Tódiłhił

tó - *water* • diłhił - *it is dark*

Dark water. This is the name of a largish lake in the Chuska Mountains (Ch'óshgai).
Whiskey is also called *tódiłhił* in Navajo, thus the use by non-Navajos of the English
name. The lake is about 10 miles north of Tohatchi (Tóhaach'i').

White Cliffs, Gallup, New Mexico: Tséyaaniigai

tsé - *rock* • yaa - *down, downward* • niigai - *white extends and stops*

White rock extends downward and stops. Situated about 3 miles to the northeast
of Gallup (Na'nízhoozhí), this massive, moon-white mesa of Cretaceous rock
dominates the tangled motif of hogback, lower lying pinyon and cedar covered
hills, large open meadows, and compact canyons. Close to the east is the red rock
frontage near Rehoboth (Tséyaaniichii'). There is much evidence in the White Cliffs
area of early Anasazi occupation.

White Cone, Arizona: Séí Heets'ósí Biką'

séí - *sand* • heets'ósí (heets'óóz) - *to be cone-shaped, conical* • biką' - *male*

Male cone-shaped sand. This tall white Chuska sandstone cone is situated 10 miles
north of Crystal (Tó Níłts'ílí) and south of Whiskey Creek (Tódiłhił). The conical
formation is also known as *Baa'oogeedí* (where it was dug into). Another White
Cone in Arizona is 12 miles north of Indian Wells (Tó Hahadleeh) and is called
Hak'eelt'izh (glans penis).

White Cone, New Mexico: **Séí Heets'ósí Bi'áád**
séí - *sand* • heets'ósí (heets'óóz) - *cone-shaped, conical* • bi'áád - *female*
Female cone-shaped sand. This sandstone cone is situated west of the Tunicha (Tó Ntsaa) escarpment and between Wheatfields (Tó Dzís'á) and Whiskey Creek (Tódiłhił). The tapered cones in both Arizona and New Mexico are of ceremonial importance to the Navajos.

Whitehorse Lake, New Mexico: **Tó Hwiisxíní**
tó - *water* • hwiisxį́ - *one was killed* • (n)í - *the place*
Where one was killed by water. The Navajo name alludes to a drowning in this lake 25 miles northeast of Crownpoint (T'iists'óóz Ńdeeshgizh). The lake is also known as *Tó Hweełhíní*, with the same interpretation. Another widely used term for the lake is *Łį́į́łgaii Be'ek'id* (literally, white horse lake).

White House Ruin, Arizona: **Kiníí' Na'ígai**
kin - *house, building* • níí' - *middle, center* • na'ígai - *a white streak across*
A house streaked across the middle with white. A yellowish-white room above the main ruin in this Canyon de Chelly (Tséyi') site is the origin of the Navajo name. The ruin is some three miles into the canyon above Chinle (Ch'ínílį́).

Whiterock, Arizona: **Tsé Ałch'į̹' Naagai**
tsé - *rock(s)* • ałch'į̹' - *come together, face each other* • naa - *downward, descend* • gai - *white*
Rocks come down together white. White rocks face each other. This spot, 18 miles northeast of Two Gray Hills (Bis Dah Łitso), in the Toadlena (Tó Háálí) area, was known, in former times, as the Knowles Store.

White Sand Comes Out, New Mexico: **Séí Hasgai**
séí - *sand* • ha - *up out, up and out* • (s)gai - *white*
Sand comes up and out white. The Navajo name defines a spot on a hill a short distance north of T&R Market (Ts'ah Bii' Ch'iyáán Bá Hooghan, Ałk'i Dah Yílk'idí) and flanking U.S. Highway 666. It is roughly 5 miles north of Gallup (Na'nízhoozhí).

Wide Belt Mesa, New Mexico: **Sis Naateel**
sis - *belt* • naa - *across, horizontal* • teel - *wide, broad*
Wide belt across. Horizontal wide belt. The mesa, isolated in country about 18 miles west of Cuba, New Mexico, was part of *Dinétah* (among the people), the old Navajo habitat, and important in Navajo ceremonialism. It is now in the southwestern township of the Jicarilla Apache Indian Reservation.

Wide Ruins, Arizona: **Kinteel**
kin - *house, building* • nteel - *wide, broad*
Wide house. The site is about 15 miles north of Chambers (Ch'ilzhóó'). The Anasazi ruins here cover some thirty acres. *Kinteel* is the Navajo term for other ruins, such as Aztec and Pueblo Pintado.

Wijiji (Wegeji), New Mexico: **Díwózhiishzhiin**
díwózhii - *greasewood* • (sh)zhiin - *black*
Black greasewood. See *Blue House, New Mexico.*

Wildcat Peak, Arizona: **Náshdóíts'ǫ'í**
náshdóí - *wildcat* • ts'ǫ' - *guts, intestines* • í - *the place*

Wildcat guts. The origin of the term is unknown. The peak of igneous rock, rising to 6,648 feet, is on Navajo land in the northwest corner of the Hopi Reservation (Ayahkinii, Oozéí).

Wildcat Trading Post, New Mexico: Náshdóí Ba'áán
náshdóí - *wildcat* • ba (bi) - *his, her, its* • a'áán - *cave*

Wildcat cave. The name alludes to wildcats formerly in the area. This abandoned trading post was about 13 miles east of Window Rock (Tségháhoodzání).

Wild Horse Mesa, Utah: Tsé Ndoolzhah
tsé - *rock* • ndoolzhah - *it comes down jagged*

Jagged rock descending. A former area where the Navajos captured wild horses, this extensive mesa is in southern Utah, 15 to 20 miles northwest of Navajo Mountain (Naatsis'áán). It is also known as the Kaiparowits Plateau.

Willow Spring, Arizona: Aba' Tó
aba' - *waiting* • tó - *water, spring*

Waiting water. The spring is 15 miles north of Cameron (Na'ní'á Hayázhí). Inscriptions and petroglyphs abound in the vicinity.

Window Rock, Arizona: Tséghahoodzání
tsé - *rock* • ghá - *through* • hoodzá - *perforated area or space* • (n)í - *the one*

The rock with a hole through it. This sandstone formation with a large wind and weather blown hole through it marks the site of the capital of the Navajo Nation. It is 25 miles northwest of Gallup (Na'nízhoozhí), New Mexico. The Navajo name is also used to define Wittick Natural Arch, Arizona and other perforated rock formations in Navajo country (Diné Bikéyah).

Windy Canyon, New Mexico: Tsé Bii' Naayolí
tsé - *rock(s)* • bii' - *in it, in them* • naayolí - *windy, wind blowing around*

Wind blowing around in the rocks. Windy Canyon is situated about 6 miles southwest of Chuska Peak (Ch'óshgai).

Winslow, Arizona: Béésh Sinil
béésh - *iron* • sinil - *they lie in position*

Iron lying in position. The Navajo name refers to stacked iron rails at Winslow, which is on the Santa Fe Railroad. Winslow is 32 miles west of Holbrook (T'iisyaakin). The town is a commercial center for Navajos, Hopis, and Anglos.

Wittick Natural Arch, Arizona: Tséghahoodzání
tsé - *rock* • ghá - *through* • hoodzá - *perforated area or space* • (n)í - *the one*

Rock with a hole through it. This large red sandstone arch is some 6 miles northwest of Cove (K'aabizhii, K'aabizhiistł'ah) in the red rock territory between the Lukachukai (Lók'a'ch'égai) and Carrizo mountains (Dził Náhoozilii). Window Rock has the same Navajo name as Wittick Natural Arch.

Wolf Crossing, Arizona: Tółchí'íkooh
tó - *water, spring* • łchí'í (łichíí') - *red, it is red* • kooh - *wash*

Red water wash. See *Toltcheco, Arizona.*

Window Rock, Arizona: Tséghahoodzáni

Wood Springs, Arizona: Tsiyi' Tóhi

tsi (tsin) - *wood(s)* • yi' - *inside, within* • tó - *water* • (h)i - *the place*

The place where there is water or a spring in the woods. The location of Wood Springs is between Ganado (Lók'aahnteel) and Nazlini (Názlíní).

Woodruff Butte, Arizona: Toohjį' Hwiidzoh

tooh - *river* • jį' - *up to it* • hwii - *space, area* • dzoh - *draw a line, a mark*

A line extending up to the river. The Navajo name depicts the line of the mesa approaching the river. Woodruff Butte is a volcanic formation sacred to the Navajos. Navajo medicine men have traditionally visited the butte to collect Jimson weed and other plants for ceremonial use. It lies about 15 miles southeast of Holbrook (T'iisyaakin) on the Little Colorado River (Tółchí'íkooh).

Wupatki, Arizona: Anaasází Bikin

anaa' - *enemy, alien, war* • sází - *ancestor* • bi - *his, her, its* • kin - *house(s)*

Houses of the enemy ancestors. This large ruin is situated 11 miles east of Highway 89 between Flagstaff (Kin Łání) and Cameron (Na'ní'á Hayázhí). The ruins are important in Hopi mythology. The Navajos began settling in the area in the 1870's.

Yale Point, Arizona: Bitsįįh Hwiits'os

bitsįįh - *its base* • hwii - *area, space* • ts'os - *it tapers*

A hill that tapers at its base. Yale Point, at an elevation of 8,050 feet, is on Black Mesa (Dziłijiin). The Navajo name refers to the contours of part of Black Mesa. The point is about 19 miles northwest of Chinle (Ch'ínílį). It was named by Gregory for Yale University.

Ya-Ta-Hey, New Mexico: T'áá Bíich'įįdii
t'áá - *just, kind of, quite* • bíí' - *in him, her, it* • ch'įįdii - *devil, ghost, evil spirit*

One who kind of has the devil in him or her. The term can be complimentarily applied to one who is a doer or go-getter. The Navajo sobriquet has been given to J.B. Tanner, who established a trading post or store about 6 miles north of Gallup (Na'nízhoozhí). A community, named *Ya-Ta-Hey* by Tanner, has grown up in the immediate area. This name is a rendition of the standard Navajo greeting *yá'át'ééh*, a third person singular verb form which means *it is good*. See *Aneth, Utah*.

Zia Pueblo, New Mexico: Tł'ógí
tł'ó - *hairy, woolly* • (g)í - *the ones*

The hairy ones. It is supposed that the *Tł'ógí Dine'é (hairy people)* clan of the Navajos originated at Zia in the 17th century when they were living in *Dinétah* (among the people), the old Navajo country around Huerfano (Dził Ná'oodiłii) and Gobernador Knob (Ch'óol'į'í), in northern New Mexico. The pueblo is some 30 miles south of Cuba (Na'azísí To'í) and about 10 miles east of Cabezon Butte (Tsé Naajiin).

Zuni Pueblo, New Mexico: Naasht'ézhí
naa' (anaa') - *enemy, enemies* • (sh)t'ézh (t'éézh) - *blacken with charcoal* • í - *the ones*

Enemies blackened with charcoal. The Navajos and Zunis were traditional enemies. Zuni warriors streaked or marked their faces and bodies with charcoal. The pueblo is 37 miles south of Gallup (Na'nízhoozhí). The magnificent mesa *Towayaalane* (Tséé'dóhdoon) rises closely to the east of the village.

Zuni Salt Lake, New Mexico: Áshįįh
áshįįh - *salt*

This salt lake southeast of Zuni Pueblo (Naasht'ézhí) and 20 miles south of Atarque (Tsélichíí', Tsé Łichíí' Sikaadí, Adáágii) has long been used by the Zunis for gathering salt. The Navajos also have procured salt from the lake from the earliest days. Navajo mythology places the lake as the home of *Áshįįh Asdzą́* (Salt Woman).

Zuni Trail, Arizona: Naasht'ézhí Haayáhí
Naasht'ézhí - *Zuni(s)* • ha(a) - *up, up out* • yá - *go on foot (singular)* • (h)í - *the place*

The place where the Zuni went up and out. This trail in Canyon de Chelly (Tséyi') is said to be the route taken by a Zuni to escape from captivity by the Navajos.

Zuni Mountains, New Mexico: Naasht'ézhí Dził
Naasht'ézhí - *Zuni(s)* • dził - *mountain(s)*

Zuni mountains, or more literally, charcoal-streaked enemy mountains. This range runs from 20 miles southeast of Gallup for nearly sixty miles to the Grants (Naatooh Sik'ai'í) area. It is heavily forested by ponderosa pine and for this reason is also called *Ńdíshchíí' Łą'í* (many pines). Many Navajos refer to it as *Tł'ohchini* (place of wild onions) because of its proximity to Ramah (Tł'ohchini), which lies a few miles to the southwest of the western part of the mountains. And one may hear it termed *Shash Bitoo'* (bear springs) by Navajos living at or in the Fort Wingate (Shash Bitoo') area, which closely borders the northern escarpments of the range.

Zuni Salt Lake, New Mexico: Áshįįh

The author and publisher join in sharing with the reader the following tradition:

The Navajos often deliberately leave small pathways in their weaving, sandpaintings, and other creations to allow freedom of movement to the spirits. They call this ch'íhóót'i' (way out), and we may invoke the concept even though such small errata as may remain in this work are entirely inadvertent.

References

Barnes, Will C.
Arizona Place Names. Tucson: University of Arizona Press, 1988.

Basso, Keith
Western Apache Language and Culture: Essays in Linguistic Anthropology. Tucson: University of Arizona Press, 1990.

Brugge, David M.
Tségai: An Archeological Ethnohistory of The Chaco Region. Washington, D.C.: U.S. Department of the Interior National Park Service, 1968.

Franciscan Fathers
An Ethnologic Dictionary of the Navajo Language. Reprinted 1968, St. Michaels Arizona: St. Michaels Press 1910.

Goodman, James M.
The Navajo Atlas: Environments, Resources, People, and History of the Diné Bikéyah. Norman: University of Oklahoma Press, 1982.

Haile, Berard
A Stem Vocabulary of the Navajo Language, Navajo-English. St. Michaels, Arizona: St. Michaels Press, 1950.
A Stem Vocabulary of the Navajo Language, English-Navajo. St. Michaels, Arizona: St Michaels Press, 1951.

Link, Martin
Navajo: A Century of Progress, 1868-1968. Flagstaff, Arizona: K.C. Publications, 1968.

Pearce, T.M.
New Mexico Place Names: A Geographical Dictionary. Albuquerque: The University of New Mexico Press, 1965.

Van Valkenburgh, Richard F.
Diné Bikéyah. Window Rock, Arizona: U.S. Department of the Interior, Bureau of Indian Affairs, 1941.

Wilson, Alan
Breakthrough Navajo. Gallup: The University of New Mexico, Gallup Branch, 1969.

Wyman, Leland C.
Blessingway. Tucson: The University of Arizona Press, 1970.

Young, Robert W. and William Morgan, Sr.
The Navajo Language, Grammar and Dictionary. Phoenix. The Bureau of Indian Affairs, 1943.
The Navajo Historical Series. Phoenix: The Bureau of Indian Affairs, 1949.
The Navajo Language: A Grammar and Colloquial Dictionary. Albuquerque: The University of New Mexico Press, 1987.

Navajo-English Glossary

Aba' Tó - Willow Spring, AZ, 69
Adáá' Dik'ą́ - Roof Butte, AZ, 48
Adah Ch'ínyáhí - Adah Chijiyahi
Canyon, AZ, 1
Adah Hosh Łání - Meteor Crater,
AZ, 36
Adahiilíní - Grand Falls, AZ, 24
Adláanii Da'ałchoozhígi - Gallup
Chamber of Commerce, Gallup,
NM, 22
Aghaałą́ - Agathla Peak (El Capitan),
AZ, 1
Aghaałą́ - El Capitan, AZ, 19
Ahideelk'id - Continental Divide,
NM, 15
Ahoyoolts'ił - Jacob's Well, AZ, 29
Ak'i Dah Nást'ání - Hosta Butte,
NM, 26
Ałnaashii Háálíní - Gallup Hogback,
Gallup, NM, 23
Ałnaashii Ha'atiin - Cross Canyon
Trail, AZ, 17
Anaa' Sin Yił Haayáhí - Trail Where
The Enemy Walked Up Singing,
AZ, 63
Anaasází Bikin - Wupatki, AZ, 70
Ane'é Tséyi' - Canyon del Muerto,
AZ, 10
Asaa'yázhí - Little Asaayi Lake,
NM, 33
Asaayi' - Asaayi, NM, 3
Asdzą́ą́ts'ósí - Azansosi Mesa, AZ, 3
Asdzání Taah Yíyá - Taylor Spring,
AZ, 59
Aseezí - Gossip Hills, NM, 24
Áshįįh - Zuni Salt Lake, NM, 71
Áshįįh Náá'á - Salt Point, NM, 49
Ata' Ha'atiin - Middle Trail Canyon,
AZ, 37
Ata' Yílk'idí - Middle Ridge, NM, 37
Atoo' Ditsxizí - Casa San Martin,
Gallup, NM, 12
Ayakin - Sichomovi, AZ, 54
Ayahkiní - Polacca, AZ, 43
Ayahkinii - Hopi Villages, AZ, 26
Ayání Bito' - Iyanbito, NM, 29
Azee' Ál'į́ Hótsaaí - Public Health
Hospital, Gallup, NM, 44

Ba'adíwei - Bodoway, AZ, 8

Báah Díilid - Fruitland, NM, 22
Báah Háálį - Bread Springs, NM, 9
Báálók'aa'í - Balukai Mesa, AZ, 4
Bááshzhinii Dziil - Jet Mountain,
CO, 29
Báyóodzin Bikéyah - Paiute Farms,
UT, 42
Bee'eldííldahsinil - Albuquerque, NM, 2
Beehai Kééhat'í - Dulce, NM, 19
Be'ek'id Baa Ahoodzání - Pinon, AZ, 43
Be'ek'id Di'níní - Groaning Lake,
AZ, 25
Be'ek'id Halchíí' - Red Lake, NM, 46
Be'ek'id Halchíí' - Red Lake, AZ, 46
Be'ek'id Halgaii - Lake Valley, NM, 32
Be'ek'id Hatsoh - Bekithatso Lake,
AZ, 4
Be'ek'id Hatsoh - Ganado Lake, AZ, 24
Be'ek'id Hóneezí - Long Lake, NM, 33
Be'ek'id Hóteelí - Mariano Lake,
NM, 35
Béésh Dich'ízhii - Cross Canyon, AZ, 17
Béésh Łichíí'ii Bigiizh - Cottonwood
Pass, NM, 15
Béésh Łichíí'ii Bigiizh - Washington
Pass, NM, 65
Béésh Sinil - Winslow, AZ, 69
Bidahóóchii' - Bidahochee, AZ, 5
Bighá'íígeedí - Tohatchi Pass, NM, 61
Bii' Haazhdiilwo'ii - The Mall, Gallup,
NM, 34
Bįįh Bito' - Deer Springs, AZ, 18
Bíina - Ignacio, CO, 28
Bikooh Hodootł'izh - Blue Canyon,
AZ, 8
Bilagáana Nééz - Counselors, NM, 16
Bíniishdáhí - Penistaja, NM, 43
Bis Dah Łitso - Two Gray Hills,
NM, 65
Bis Deez'áhí - Newcomb, NM, 40
Bis Dootł'izh Deez'áhí - Round Rock
Trading Post, AZ, 49
Bisóodi Sidáhí - Sitting Pig, NM, 55
Bistahí - Bisti, NM, 6
Bitát'ah Dzígai - Marsh Pass, AZ, 35
Bitát'ahkin - Betatakin, AZ, 4
Bitł'ááh Bito' - Beclabito, AZ, 4
Bitsįįh Hwiits'os - Yale Point, AZ, 70

Chéch'iizh Bii' Tó - Ojo Encino, NM, 41

79

Tsiizizii - Leupp, AZ, 33
Tsin Bił Dah Azkání - Howell Mesa,
    AZ, 27
Tsin Łeeh Yí'áhí - Mocking Bird
    Canyon, NM, 37
Tsin Názbąs - Smith Lake, NM, 56
Tsin Sikaad - Tsin Sikaad, AZ, 64
Tsinaabąąs Habitiin - Coppermine,
    AZ, 15
Tsinaabąąs Habitiin - The Gap, AZ, 60
Tsinyi' Be'ek'id - Forest Lake, AZ, 21
Tsiyi' Tóhí - Wood Springs, AZ, 70
Tsoodził - Mount Taylor, NM, 38
Tsoodził- San Mateo Peak, NM, 51
Tsosts'id Be'ek'id - Seven Lakes,
    NM, 53

Ts'ah Bii' Ch'iyáán Bá Hooghan - T&R
    Market, near Gallup, NM, 59,
Ts'ah Bii' Kin - Inscription House,
    AZ, 28
Ts'ah Bii' Njik'ai'í - Sagebrush Liquors
    (northwest of Gallup), NM, 49
Ts'íhootso - St. Michaels, AZ, 57
Ts'í'mah - Chama, NM, 13

Yaaniilk'id - Cedar Ridge, AZ, 12
Yaaniilk'id - Gap, AZ, 24
Ya'niilzhiin - Torreon, NM, 62
Yé'iitsoh Bidił Niníyęęzh - Anzac,
    NM, 2
Yisdá Dziil - Cache Mountain, NM, 9
Yootó - Santa Fe, NM, 52